For Randy —
You have always lived large!
Elizabeth B. Crook
2018

LIVE LARGE

THE ACHIEVER'S GUIDE
TO WHAT'S NEXT

ELIZABETH B. CROOK

GREENLEAF
BOOK GROUP PRESS

This publication is designed to provide accurate and authoritative information in regard to the subject matter covered. It is sold with the understanding that the publisher and author are not engaged in rendering legal, accounting, or other professional services. If legal advice or other expert assistance is required, the services of a competent professional should be sought.

The names and identifying characteristics of persons referenced in this book have been changed to protect their privacy.

Published by Greenleaf Book Group Press
Austin, Texas
www.gbgpress.com

Distributed by Greenleaf Book Group

For ordering information or special discounts for bulk purchases, please contact Greenleaf Book Group at PO Box 91869, Austin, TX 78709, 512.891.6100.

Design and composition by Greenleaf Book Group
Cover design by Greenleaf Book Group
All photos should include a credit line adjacent to the photo:
©Yuriy2012, 2016. Used under license from Shutterstock.com;
©iStockphoto.com/aarows

Cataloging-in-Publication data is available.

Print ISBN: 978-1-62634-415-0

eBook ISBN: 978-1-62634-416-7

Part of the Tree Neutral® program, which offsets the number of trees consumed in the production and printing of this book by taking proactive steps, such as planting trees in direct proportion to the number of trees used: www.treeneutral.com

Printed in the United States of America on acid-free paper

17 18 19 20 21 22   10 9 8 7 6 5 4 3 2 1

First Edition

Advance Praise

"If you are an achiever who has been waiting for that next big thing—if you have felt the call for a larger life—then this book is for you. Elizabeth Crook is the career guide for those who thought they had it all. *Live Large: The Achiever's Guide to What's Next* is the book 2017 has been waiting for. I highly recommend it!"

—**Jane Pauley**, Host of *CBS Sunday Morning* and
Author of *Your Life Calling*

"Are you an achiever ready for your next big step? Are you ready to live fully and authentically without limits or constraints? *Live Large: The Achiever's Guide to What's Next* will not only align you with your true purpose, it is one of the most thrilling ways to go after what you want to accomplish and make a difference in the world. Elizabeth Crook is the real deal, and delivers great value in this book."

—**Jack Canfield**, Coauthor of the #1 *New York Times* Bestselling *Chicken Soup for the Soul®* Series and *The Success Principles*™

"You're successful, yet you feel that there's something more for you. The challenge is that you don't know what that 'something more' is, how to find out, or how to get there. Let Elizabeth Crook's remarkable book, *Live Large: The Achiever's Guide to What's Next*, be your guide. This book combines Elizabeth's insight as a business strategist with her genuine love of people to help you find your way to the next, quite possibly most fulfilling, stage in your life and career. *Live Large* isn't just a great resource—it's a treasure."

—**Joe Calloway**, Author of *Becoming A Category Of One*

"In my field, I often come across successful business folks looking for their next big horizon. Elizabeth Crook, an accomplished CEO herself, who has helped build so many career success stories, has finally created the astonishingly effective Live Large process that moves you to your next great step. You will walk away from this 'playbook' forever changed in the best way possible!"

—**Verne Harnish**, CEO of Gazelles, Author of *Scaling Up: How a Few Companies Make It . . . and Why the Rest Don't*

"Elizabeth tackles the question of 'What's Next' for successful people ready for a new challenge. A big paycheck can feel hollow when disconnected from purpose. Elizabeth guides her readers back to their core strengths so that they can Live Large in their careers and personal lives."

—**Amanda Steinberg**, CEO of Daily Worth

"*Live Large* is a practical and wise guide that integrates inner exploration with real-world grit . . . an inspiring and easy-to-follow roadmap for personal and professional growth."

—Marc Lesser, Author of *Less: Accomplishing More By Doing Less* and *Know Yourself, Forget Yourself*

"Elizabeth Crook captures the spirit of the entrepreneur in *Live Large*: that restlessness to see more, know more, be more. She illuminates for the reader a pathway to unlock our potential to do more than we ever imagined."

—Michael Burcham, Founding CEO of Nashville Entrepreneur Center; Faculty, Owen Graduate School of Management, Vanderbilt; Serial Entrepreneur

"*Live Large* is for anyone who has already successfully achieved many of their life goals but may be just beginning to look at what's next in terms of making more of an impact and possibly even changing direction. Elizabeth's process will help you look back to look forward, be honest about who you are and who you are becoming, and create a life lived with purpose and intention."

—Pat Obuchowski, Founder of Gutsy Women Win and Author of *Gutsy Women Win: How to Get Gutsy and Get Going*

"Elizabeth's wise, conversational, and meaningful words inspire me to look deep inside, to reflect, to act, and to ultimately Live Large. I have no doubt that this book, and this process, will help successful people become even more successful and change lives for good."

—Janet Miller, CEO/Market Leader of Colliers International

"I'm so excited to see this book coming to fruition! Elizabeth is a wise, experienced leader who has helped me in so many ways and has delivered big time whenever I refer her to others. She has been an essential part of my success, and I'm confident readers will say the same after reading through and engaging with the pearls of wisdom and practical insights contained in this volume."

—Joel Solomon, Chair, Renewal Funds; Chair, Hollyhock; Author of *The Clean Money Revolution*

To Lisa Quin Lorimer Donahue

"The real voyage of discovery consists
not in seeking new landscapes, but in having new eyes."
—Marcel Proust

"The mind, once stretched by a new idea,
never returns to its original dimensions."
—Ralph Waldo Emerson

CONTENTS

Section III: Your Big, Beautiful Life

FOREWORD

At the time of writing this, I'm 52 years old, and I've been into personal development since I was a teenager. I've read hundreds of self-help books and attended tens of thousands of hours of personal-development training. In fact, I teach this subject to others and have written several books myself. As the host of the popular iTunes podcast *The Mind Aware Show*, I've interviewed over 300 thought leaders from around the world. Believe me—I have seen and heard it all, and this I can tell you: *Live Large* and its message stand out.

In March of 2013, I was sitting in the living room of Jack Canfield's house with 16 other eager future authors. We were piled on the big cushy sofas with the *Chicken Soup for the Soul* creator himself, as well as one of the stars of the runaway hit movie, *The Secret*. All of us waited with bated breath for our turn in the "hot seat": the chair at the front of the room next to Jack. Over the next two days, each of us would take a seat in that chair, talk about our respective books, and get advice from the man himself.

It was in this room that I met Elizabeth Crook.

Every person in the room was already successful in their particular arenas of life, and—speaking candidly—we had all paid a pretty penny to be there. (By "pretty penny," I mean a sum of money that is large enough to make you embarrassed to say it aloud, for fear that you look like a groupie or just plain crazy to pay that type of money for a couple days in someone's living room.) The reason I mention the expense is to stress the point that this was a room of heavyweights. This was a room of achievers. This was a room full of people who were stars in their respective fields, and in this room, Elizabeth shined the brightest.

When she took her turn in the hot seat, Elizabeth talked about her father's success and about her own . . . and then she said something that made everyone lean forward: "I see things differently than other people. I see patterns. I can look at a person's business or life, and I can connect the dots. I don't know how I do it . . . I just do it. I've always been able to see these patterns, and that is my gift."

From that point forward, Elizabeth became the darling of the event, with everyone clamoring to talk with her about their businesses and their lives, asking for advice on how to "connect the dots." And she delivered.

I had my first of many personal "Aha!" moments during my discussions with Elizabeth over those two days. And in our countless conversations since that time, I've had the opportunity to observe who she is and why *Live Large* is such an important piece of work. First, she has spent decades working with powerful men—and they *listen* to her. CEOs and other achievers, men who are used to getting advice from, well, other men. In a culture that often doesn't value women's voices, Elizabeth's is heard. This is a testament to both the strength of her message and her ability to convey that message in a way that truly connects with anyone.

Second, she's *lived*. Her full life has been defined by many transformative experiences, and when she draws from them in *Live Large*, you immediately connect to her story. She's not just giving you advice—she uses her own experiences to give insights into what's moved her forward in life, and what might move you forward in yours.

Finally, Elizabeth is an original. *Live Large* is not regurgitated material written in a different voice. The Explorations in this book are fresh and one-of-a-kind. In the ocean of material that is available to us today, Elizabeth's book gives you ideas that are new and endlessly effective.

Live Large is more than just a book, or a workbook: It's the workbook of *you*. By completing the Explorations outlined in this book, you will rediscover yourself, and you will realize that you already possess everything you need to take your life to the next level. Just like Dorothy in *The Wizard of Oz*, you've had it all along. Elizabeth simply helps you discover what "it" is and how to put it to good use.

It's always fun to have an "aha" moment, but it's even more fun to have a dozen of them. If you know that life has more in store for you, and you're ready to step up and be the person you know you were meant to be, then *Live Large* is the map you need—and Elizabeth is your ultimate guide.

—Dana Wilde, bestselling author of *Train Your Brain*
and Host of *The Mind Aware Show*

Imagine the Unimaginable

Perhaps you've surprised yourself by buying this book. You've lived a life people point to as successful: You've made the "right" decisions, reached the goals you set out to, achieved status in your industry, and been rewarded or acknowledged for your accomplishments. But while you have every reason to feel content, instead you feel restless. You want to know what's next. To someone who has already reached a high level of success, this question may seem risky, unreasonable, and immature . . . not to mention far out of reach. The answer would surely lead you to that wider horizon you believe might be around the corner, but between you and that horizon lies an abyss that feels too dangerous to cross.

The truth is, the wide horizon you are imagining is right in front of you. You only have to discover the path that leads you there. This book will show you how. We all have limitations on what we can imagine. It's time to imagine the unimaginable.

I've been right where you are before. And I've walked this road many times with people just like you: smart, successful people who were struggling with doubt about their next steps, about whether they really could achieve the greatness they held as a vision in their mind's eye. Once these achievers were led through the Live Large process outlined in the pages of this book, they experienced the miracle of being able to move beyond a life that had begun to feel limiting and toward one of fulfillment, joy, and living (very) large.

Live Large is a book about intention: the intention to honor that "what's next" feeling and to move forward even though you have already achieved so much. It is about exploring and acknowledging the depth of your talents and experiences and discovering how to use these abundant personal resources to align yourself with an even deeper purpose.

You may think, "Well, it's easy for her to say, she's already doing what she loves." This is true: I am one of the most fortunate people I know. Using my experience and unique set of inborn and cultivated gifts, I work with high achievers who support my creativity and are looking to generate positive influence in the world. In short, most of the time I am working exactly the way I have always wanted to with exactly the people I've always wanted around me. But it wasn't always like that.

In my midforties, I was a senior executive at a software company. We were on the bleeding edge, developing expert systems and working long, crazy hours. It was exhilarating. I loved the challenge of structuring a new company, positioning products, closing big contracts, and pitching the story to investors.

Then, about four years into it, the company started to go in a direction I believed would lead to failure. Eventually I found myself in a messy, political fight. Could I have "won"? Who knows?

Does it matter? Not really. What does matter is that one day, when I was driving home from the airport after *yet another* trade show, I realized I was working way too hard for something that I simply didn't care about—yet I was living as if I did.

Leave-taking is almost always messy. At first I was stunned. I had jumped off a train going a hundred miles an hour and hadn't waited for it to slow down. The landing hurt. What was I supposed to do with all of my full-speed energy? And what about my identity? I loved being able to say what I did professionally. I felt important and powerful. What now?

Luckily, the company repurchased my options, affording me time to consider what to do next. I wandered, wallowed, explored. I cried a lot. I wanted to find a new professional path—one that truly mattered to me—but I didn't have a clue where to look. I would love to be able to tell you *the light dawned*, *I just knew*, or *I talked to an expert*, but that's not what happened. Instead, as a forty-something looking to build a career from scratch, I felt *old*. I loved health and healing, but that was my father's gig. I was living in Nashville, where everyone was creating or producing music, but I felt my age precluded my pursuing something similar.

And then I took a good, hard look at my father. He was in his seventies and still going strong as a pediatrician who had founded an innovative medical clinic. In his late fifties, he'd decided to write books that would help people live healthier lives. At sixty-nine, he wrote a book called *The Yeast Connection* that sold over a million copies. He also worked to get sugar out of baby food, and wrote and spoke passionately about how nutrition played a key role in a child's physical and emotional health. He was nearly thirty years older than I was at that point. Suddenly I stopped wallowing and thought: "If I work at something I love as long as he has, then I have at least thirty years to do something!" I had plenty of time. But what was it I wanted to do?

Like so many other soul searchers, I turned inward, became interested in the mind, body, and spirit connection and my own intuition. Around this time, a holistic healthcare trend was beginning to take shape far out on the horizon. Deepak Chopra, Larry Dossey, Dean Ornish, Patch Adams, and others had come on the scene, and even at this early stage, I could sense the power of the movement. Coming from a long line of physicians—from my great-grandfather and grandfather down to my uncle and my father—I used to joke that my family was "into health" before it became a national obsession. Though not a physician myself, I worked at Planned Parenthood as the director of volunteers and later as a public information officer for the State Health Department. Given my history, I thought health might be my next chapter.

Like so many people who think just one more course or one more degree will give us the ticket to dance, I was pretty sure I needed to go back to school to get more letters behind my name in order to garner attention for this work. A few months later, however, at a conference where the highest pantheon of integrative physicians and practitioners were speaking, I met a physician whose words shifted my thinking entirely. When I told her I was going back to school to make a difference, she said, "Don't you think we have enough practitioners? If you want to make a difference in the world, do what you do best."

We all hear about "aha" moments, and this was one of mine. Careers or professional paths aside, *what did I do best?*

As I pondered that question, I was reminded of a phone call I received many years earlier, while I lived and worked in Caracas, Venezuela. It was a very different place then than now—safe, prosperous, sophisticated. While working as vice president of systems development and training, I received a call from a large international search firm. When they told me they were looking for someone to open a chain of doughnut franchises, I was completely bewildered. I didn't have food experience, consumer product experience, or franchise experience. On top of that, I don't even like doughnuts!

Unable to mask my confusion, I asked the caller on the other end of the line: *Why me?* The caller explained there was no one in Venezuela that had all the required experience for the position. Still confused, I asked, *So what were your search criteria?* "Oh," he replied, "we looked for people who had a record of success doing things that have never been done before."

This answer changed my understanding of my professional identity forever.

It was the first time in my life I knew what tied together all the things I had done to that point. Some people hear music and write poetry. I saw patterns, frameworks, and themes. I knew how to create what had not existed before. I knew how to fit pieces together to make things work better. I don't know how I knew to do this, I just did. Because of this, people were always asking me for advice about how to think and plan for what was next in their career and in their businesses. I engaged in these conversations naturally even before I realized that was what I was doing, but once I contemplated the physician's words—do what you do best—I became more aware, accepting, and intentional in using this talent.

I began interviewing those who asked for advice about their lives: what sang for them, what they had learned and been challenged by. Then we would explore the limitations that might be holding them back, and the balance between risk and reward. We talked about how frustrated they could be or excited they could get about their definitions of themselves. And then we brainstormed what they most wanted. By exploring their deepest desires, people started to see their own themes and patterns. The process freed them from their job titles and industries and let them claim who they always wanted to be. I didn't have the answers—they did! And they used these answers to create a life they loved. After embracing my passion for facilitating others to find answers that worked for them, helping them to see possibilities in both individual and group settings, I started my own company, now known as Orchard Advisors. Orchards, after all, are places where things grow and thrive.

As the founder and CEO of my company, I work coast to coast and internationally with companies and company leaders to help them find fresh approaches, reach brand new levels of success, and become more effective at what they do. I knew this work had a powerful spark all its own when I was asked to speak to my first group of CEOs, all of whom were men. I already knew women could share—it's what we do. But I worried the guys would look at me like I was crazy when I suggested they turn to the person sitting next to them and talk about their insights and fears. Instead, they were completely focused on either speaking or listening. You could feel the connection, the excitement in the room. What a surprise!

I've since facilitated this process with attorneys, back-to-the-workforce moms, entrepreneurs, artists, and CEOs in workshops, boardrooms, and one-on-ones. I do it as a prelude to company strategic planning and in personal exploration sessions. I do it for million-dollar companies, and I do it for hundred-million-dollar companies. And it's changed lives. A philanthropist became part of a groundbreaking team to help entrepreneurs create values-based businesses; a high-end men's retail manager started running a gallery/gathering place for artists and art lovers that became a social center of her city; a CEO partnered with an executive he admired and started his own business with plenty of time to see his family.

What Live Large Means

Live Large is an invitation, a challenge, an imperative, even a dare to embrace the entirety of who we are, and to create a life of potency and inspiration. It captures the celebratory feeling of affirmation that we are using our greatest gifts and talents to do work that energizes us and makes an impact. When we are living large, we get to throw our arms in the air and feel excited and inspired about what we do. So, whenever you see the words "Live Large" in this book, remember that it represents not only the invitation, but also the goal you are moving toward: a state of engagement and deep satisfaction.

At forty-six, I never felt unique enough, special enough, wildly talented enough (oh, maybe sometimes), or young enough to start anything life changing. I have come to realize that I am enough of all those things—and so are you. I have been called an irreverent, sometimes outrageous strategist, corporate shaman, witch doctor, mapmaker, magician, and coach, but whatever my title, I am doing what I love. *And you can too.*

That's why *Live Large* was born, to offer this process to you, to reassure you that—yes!—you are unique enough, special enough, wildly talented enough, and at exactly the right stage in life to walk confidently toward that wide horizon. This interactive, self-searching, tried-and-true process will lead you down the road toward loving who you are and what you do, and living the life you've always imagined.

Seeing in Technicolor: How to Use This Book

For an achiever, moving toward the next step in life can be both wildly exciting and a little terrifying, because we are not people who tend to take next steps lightly. We try to make a noticeable impact in whatever arena we are traversing. *Live Large* not only honors your intention to take this step, it provides you with a detailed map to help you determine what is calling you. Below you will find a summary of that map and the journey you are about to take. This will give you a sense of how the process will unfold and where you will find yourself at each juncture of the book. Remember: I have led hundreds of people from all walks of life through this process. I have never seen it fail. You are about to begin the beautiful work of finding how to live larger than you ever have before.

People who experience the most dramatic shifts during this process are often the ones who lean into their growing edge. Marshall Goldsmith is an internationally recognized coach and author who, like me, works with achievers like you—people who have experienced successes both large and small. The title of his bestselling book captures it in a phrase: *What Got You Here Won't Get You There*. We all have the tendency to double down on the styles, habits, and ways of relating to both others and ourselves that have served us well in the past. However, if any of us are truly going to Live Large, now is the time to challenge some of those behaviors.

In other words, "leaning into" our growing edge means examining what's worked and what hasn't, and being open to fresh approaches. For those of you who push yourselves relentlessly and are demanding and impatient for results, see what it's like to take a more laid-back approach. If you are someone who tends to relax back and let things happen, you might use this time to push harder. The natural tendency is to pay attention to anything that reinforces our natural inclination. Take a look at your growing edge, or the opposite of what you usually do. It might be exactly the thing that leads you toward a richer life.

A Preview of Your Adventure

Some years ago, I went hiking in Patagonia, in the southernmost part of Chile. Before leaving home, our guide sent a detailed description of our planned route, outlining the *refugios* where we would sleep, which days we'd experience significant vertical changes, and which days we'd take it easy. It was reassuring to know beforehand the challenges—and the beauty—that awaited us on our journey.

Climbing a mountain is a useful metaphor to give you a preview of your Live Large journey: As you climb the mountain you get a clear view of the countryside, the territory where you will see new opportunities, ones you are unlikely to see if you don't begin the adventure. Below is a description of the route you'll take to get there:

Section I: Beginning the Climb

Section I marks the beginning of the trail that will eventually lead you to the top of the mountain. You feel apprehensive but excited and energized to be here . . . perhaps you also feel a sense of freedom in stepping outside your comfort zone and daily routines. The landscape is still level—no big climbs just yet. This early portion of your journey is all about getting a feel for what's to come and learning more about the tools you'll have at your disposal.

Section I truly sets the foundation for your incredible adventure. The chapters within will help you to better understand the complexity of your life by revealing the characteristics that make you who you are. You will gain a better understanding of what holds you back (your "Triple Js") and what (and who!) propels you forward (your "Better Angels"). Critical Live Large explorations like "The Retrospective" and "The Lifeline" will help you to create a picture of who you have been over time. You will see how you have survived adversity, fear, and sadness; explore your highs, lows, and turning points; and ultimately uncover the singular purpose and the hidden values that have driven you forward.

Section II: The Steep Ascent

In Section II, your steep climb to the top begins. As you dive into a deep and profound exploration of your life, you may hear a voice that questions whether this type of reflection is a good idea. Don't worry: It is common to feel hesitant in the face of transformation. Although your pace may slow a bit, there is no doubt this challenging ascent will ultimately exhilarate an achiever like you.

The chapters in this section will introduce you to the world of possibilities that await you once you learn to let go of generational and timeworn convictions. You will learn to identify limiting patterns, stubborn dichotomies, and vicious cycles that no longer serve you. At the same time, you will be able to better understand and recognize the wealth of material already available at your fingertips to help you begin to shape the next stage of your life.

As the clouds part and the summit finally emerges, the view will be unlike anything you've ever seen: This is when you'll realize how much you know, what energizes you, and how innately gifted and wildly talented you really are. You've put in some hard work . . . now you're ready to finally soar.

Section III: Soaring to New Heights

As you enter Section III, inviting horizons begin to take shape. Now that you've reached the peak, the bird's-eye perspective gives you the opportunity to see not only the trail you left, but a network of all new trails, each leading to an exciting new destination. This section is about spotting the path you want to pursue and floating down from the peak to walk it with confidence.

These chapters will help you decide what you want to be, have, and accomplish, and what impact you want to make on the world. You will learn to clearly define what you really want in your career and what characteristics are essential for your ideal situation.

As this last section comes to a close, you'll become empowered to leave the map of the book behind and become the cartographer of your own life. You can always come back to the map again when you need help finding a sense of direction or charting new territory. Remember: Once you've reached the highest peak, you'll always have access to that bird's-eye view when you need it.

Explorations

Live Large features a number of exercises I call "Explorations" to guide you through this exciting journey. Some will be easy while others will be more challenging—especially those that challenge you to overcome your Limiting Beliefs. Some explorations may look familiar: You may have read about them or even completed them before. That is perfectly all right. What matters is that you have never been the same *you* as you are in this particular place and time.

Follow the pointers below as you complete your explorations, and I promise: You will gain new insights:

- You cannot fail, but you have to be present to win. Just show up.

- When an exploration feels hard, it may be a point of resistance—a kernel of you that is afraid to explore when change is kicking against you. When you feel this resistance, dive in! This is an invitation to use your growing edge to challenge what you've done in the past.

- Don't feel ashamed or embarrassed about your answers. Just be honest. Remember, this is a private conversation with yourself. No one will see it unless you choose to share.

- If you feel overwhelmed, just pause! Do as much as feels valuable to you, then pick back up where you left off. Read through the book at a pace that suits you best—but whatever you do, keep moving forward. You'll thank yourself for it later.

Check into our website for additional ideas or encouragement at www.elizabethbcrook.com. You can also download all the Explorations at www.elizabethbcrook.com/explorations.

If you're wondering whether you can get results from the book if you just read straight through and skip the explorations, I ask you to consider the following story. My father and his four siblings grew up during the Great Depression. Going to a "picture show" was too extravagant, so my grandmother would walk the children downtown to the theater, where they would gaze up at the full-sized movie poster along with a dozen still shots on display. My father confessed to me when I was a child that he'd thought "going to the movies" meant looking at the pictures from outside the theater.

It makes you want to smile a small, sad smile, doesn't it? Of course, they had an entertaining afternoon, spent time together as a family, even had fun. It was a peek into another world . . . but suppose they had been able to actually *go inside* and receive the full experience rather than just a tiny representation of it? How much more memorable might it have been?

If you read this book from cover to cover without engaging in the explorations, you will find something useful and valuable for your life. But if you choose to deep-dive into the explorations in each chapter and immerse yourself in the glorious living Technicolor of the full experience, *Live Large* will lead you toward the wonderful, wide-open vistas of possibility.

When you make the intentional decision to reach your fullest potential, there's nowhere to go but up—and I will be with you the whole beautiful ride.

TIP: Some people may choose to work through the book with a trusted friend. You can ask this friend to help you see characteristics that you are too modest to write down. You can each be the other's mirror. Even if you are working through the book on your own, there are some explorations in particular where you may want to seek out a trusted supporter or mentor to get their perspective. I will mark those exercises with a mirror symbol. Tell your trusted friend they are only allowed to point out positive characteristics—that you are doing the negative on your own!

SECTION

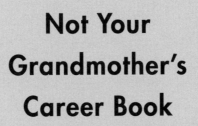

Not Your Grandmother's Career Book

"The thing that is really hard, and really amazing, is giving up on being perfect and beginning the work of becoming yourself."
—Anna Quindlen

"It's a helluva start, being able to recognize what makes you happy."
—Lucille Ball

"There is almost no such thing as ready. There is only now. And you may as well do it now. Generally speaking, now is as good a time as any."
—Hugh Laurie

"Find what makes your heart sing and create your own music."
—Mac Anderson

CHAPTER 1

The Triple J and Your Better Angels

When I was younger, I was an excellent student. But when it came to big school projects, I would get overwhelmed if I didn't know exactly what I was going to do and how I was going to do it before I began. One night, my father sat down next to me while I was in a tailspin and said, "Just think about the Zephyr." I wiped my eyes and looked at him. "The *what?*" "The Zephyr. It's a train that goes two thousand miles, all the way from Chicago to San Francisco. Do you think the engineer waits until *all* the lights between Chicago and California are green before he leaves? Of course not. All he needs is the next green light."

By picking up this book, you've made the first move toward living large. At this early stage, however, your initial enthusiasm may be met with feelings of trepidation: The challenges ahead appear daunting, possibly insurmountable, and certainly overwhelming.

When those feelings rise up in your throat, I encourage you to remember my father's wise advice: You don't need to have it all figured out just yet. You only need to make it to the next green light. The goal of this book is to help you break down this dramatic, life-changing journey into smaller, more manageable parts so that your path feels organic and fluid. Not overwhelming you is part of the process.

With that in mind, what better place to start the journey than exploring those initial feelings in depth? This first chapter will take a closer look into the thought processes and emotions that so often hold us back, as well as those that propel us forward. I like to call these your Triple J and your Better Angels. Let's dive in!

The Triple J

We all have flaws and fears we wish we could do away with. Often, the flaws are much tinier than we make them out to be—one wormhole in an otherwise perfect apple. Yet we feel disproportionately ashamed of them because we are afraid that these are the traits, rather than our positive attributes, that truly define us. We believe that as long as we possess these negative characteristics—impatience, selfishness, stubbornness, the list goes on—we will never be able to live the life that is waiting for us.

Other times we fear we are *not enough*, or *too much*, but never *just right*. We may feel too young or too old. We feel we have too much experience or not enough. We feel that it's too early or too late to make a move, and that the move we are contemplating is too big or not big enough.

These feelings and beliefs are fed by a self-defeating voice inside your head I like to call the Triple J: your Jury, your Judge, and your Jailer. It hears evidence against you and your dreams, judges those dreams, and then jails you, limiting your ability to act. Disguised as "reason," the Triple J gives you rules to live by—rules that prevent you from knowing how powerful you really are and keep you from looking further afield.

This voice is often rooted in a skepticism or disapproval that originated from a parent, teacher, sibling, friend, or coach. Even if the person is long gone, you've incorporated their voice into your thoughts, and it pops up again and again. Other times the voice develops in response to bad times and heavy disappointments. It tells you to be cautious because you've made mistakes before.

Recognizable by its negative tone, your Triple J may say things like: "You're dreaming if you think you can do that." "It's supposed to be hard, that's why they call it 'work.'" "This job I have is the only thing I really know how to do, and it's too late to change that now!" "I don't have a *real* talent in the area I want to work, and it's too late to develop it." "Changing at this stage would be too risky." This voice tries to convince you that you have to wait until:

- You get your next promotion.

- You've saved X amount of dollars.

- You've gotten married (or divorced).

- You've sold your business.

- You've lost twenty pounds.

- You're clear about exactly what you want to do.

- You've paid off your mortgage.

- Your last child has left home.

This is what the Triple J sounds like when it's fanning your fears. Ultimately, your Triple J tries to convince you there's too much at stake to make big changes. In fact, there is too much at stake not to. Your passion is at stake, your creativity, and maybe most importantly, your health—both physical and mental. The truth is, you are ready—right now—to do what you love. And unlike what this voice would tell you, you don't have to figure it out all at once.

Sometimes the Triple J focuses on our imperfections—and we all have them. Our fear is that these imperfections describe all of who we are. Because we feel so much judgment, we tend to run from any identification with these negative characteristics instead of acknowledging, "I can be stubborn sometimes, but that doesn't make me a stubborn person."

Once you recognize your Triple J for what it is, you might be tempted to shut it up when it starts to point out that you are being impatient or selfish. Instead, try taking a more curious approach. Ask yourself: Is there an opportunity here to be more patient? To be more giving? Accepting that opportunity does not mean you are selfish or impatient, that's just the concern we unconsciously hold. When we make the voice of the Triple J conscious and explicit, we can't be ruled and limited by something that is only partially true, no longer true, or was never true. In Chapter 9 you'll learn more about how this dynamic gets set up in your life and, more importantly, how to deal with it!

An Rx Antibiotic for the Triple J:

Below is an antibiotic for your Triple J, with example answers outlined in italics:

1. Make the voice of your Triple J visible or audible by either saying it aloud or writing it down.

   "I feel selfish for wanting to have a career that really satisfies me."

2. Listen or look at what it's saying and ask what evidence supports the negative belief or thought.

   "My mother used to say I was selfish because I always wanted my way when I was younger."

3. Now, ask what evidence refutes it.

   "My friends tell me I'm too considerate and that I should take more time for myself."

4. Compare the supporting and refuting evidence, and ask your highest self which evidence is more compelling.

   "When I think about it, I am a generous person and take other people's needs into account."

5. Develop an action plan based on this assessment.

   "I have talents I haven't taken time to really use. It's not selfish to want to explore doing that now."

The negativity of our Triple J scares us into staying in one place, but once we take a closer look, we see that this "monster in the room" is really just a jacket thrown over the chair. Remember: It's your birthright to love what you do and to use the skills, experience, expertise, and insights you've worked so hard to acquire to take the next step. Don't let your Triple J hold you back.

Your Better Angels

The term "Better Angels" comes from Lincoln's first inaugural address, when factions of our country were preparing for war against one another. He called on the "better angels of our nature" to, in short, form a union. Free from the self-doubt and misery of the Triple J, the voice of our Better Angels enlivens and praises us, reminds us what is good and right about who we are, and unifies the warring parts of ourselves so that we feel solid and sure in our journey toward our goal. "Great idea!" "You earned that." "You can experiment with that." "The worst that can happen is not really bad." It's true you should get curious about the Triple J and what hidden dogma it may be hiding tucked into the black cloaks of its negativity. But you should listen with unhesitating belief to your Better Angels. They understand your goodness and are here to give you strength.

We tend to listen to our Triple J and not our Better Angels for the same reason abused spouses sometimes cling to the very ones who make their lives miserable. It's easier to stick with the devil we know. And the Triple J tends to be louder.

Finding Your Guide

Because of the difficulty of listening to our Better Angels over our Triple J, it is helpful to have a trusted guide who can affirm that positive voice inside and who can accompany, encourage, and challenge you . . . someone who will warn you about what's ahead and give you the tools to move through those obstacles right when you feel like giving up. I will be your guide as you work through this book, but you may also want your own personal guide who can act as a touchstone when you run into resistance or your Triple J.

Guides are committed and loyal. They are safe and a little further ahead of you on the road you want to take. They are like Sam, the ski coach I met during a vacation in Whistler, where the 2010 Winter Olympics were held. I was a non-skier until my fifties. Being from the south, I'd rarely been able to ski more than three days a season, so I always took lessons whenever I went. Sporting a wild-colored jacket, pants, and goggles, Sam was easy to follow anywhere on the mountain. He was my guide, and he was totally committed to my success. He challenged me when my nerves failed. He knew I could do it. He showed me better ways to do things, and how old (and bad) habits were slowing me down. When I felt scared or discouraged, he reassured me so I could regain composure. In short, he was the one who supported me as I skied down slopes I never dreamed I could ski. By the end of the day, I was even able to ski part of the Dave Murray Downhill, the black diamond run used for the men's Olympic Downhill!

I later noticed that even when Sam wasn't physically with me, I could still hear his voice in my head. Whenever I felt disoriented or hesitant about a new slope, his beneficent guiding voice encouraged me to move ahead with confidence. I encourage you to find your Sam—your unwavering guide—to guide you toward the voice of your Better Angels. Trust that he or she is your ally, and call on them whenever you feel disoriented or overwhelmed.

Arriving, and Arriving Again

When you're having trouble hearing the voice of your Better Angels over that of your Triple J, you may find yourself consulting your guide over and over. Does that mean you are failing or "not doing it right"? Absolutely not.

I've taken half a dozen workshops with the well-known yoga instructor Rodney Yee. As he helps his students adjust their postures in practice (and yes, there's a reason it's called yoga practice), Rodney often reminds them that an individual never finishes or completes a yoga pose; rather, they arrive in the pose again and again. So it is with this work. As we begin the journey toward living large, our job is to become fully conscious of that which stands in our way—our Triple J—and turn instead toward our Better Angels, using our guide for help. As we practice this, we will arrive, and then arrive, and then arrive again. We are always making subtle adjustments.

I have worked with hundreds of people who wanted to grow a business, start new careers, resolve conflicts, gain mastery, feel more effective, and discover fresh perspectives. Young, old, and in the middle, executives, social workers, tech geeks, and artists all have come through enlivened and more insightful. I haven't lost anyone yet.

CHAPTER 2

Flying in Your Personal Time Machine: The Retrospective

A big part of taking the next step is first going back to find out where you have been. Great chess players, poker players, and bridge players all study and learn from past games. Great generals study military history, and great athletes review the tapes. In this chapter we will take a journey—a Retrospective—back into your life in order to give you the power to move you forward to what's next.

You may be saying: "I already know where I've been . . . I want to figure out where I'm going. Why would I look back instead of forward?" Think of the Retrospective as your present self interviewing your past self with great curiosity and compassion. When you allow yourself the opportunity to look back as an objective observer on past situations, activities, and relationships, it's easier to recognize threads that have served you well or have entangled you (we don't want them to entangle you again) and identify the themes of your life so that you can weave new futures either using or letting go of the patterns that have held you back.

What do I mean by threads, themes, and patterns? If you were the kid who loved getting everyone out to play "kick the can" in the summers or could easily convince friends to join you in getting into mischief, you will likely see the thread of leadership appear at different points in your Retrospective. Similarly, if school was a struggle but you ended up getting multiple degrees, you will see the thread of determination. With the benefit of distance, themes will begin to emerge out of these various threads. You may discover that:

- You can take ideas and make them happen.

- You have a strong internal sense of direction.

- You are willing to experiment.

- You are both patient and impatient.

The Retrospective is an incredibly important foundational tool for helping you recognize and bust out of any old patterns you no longer want to keep, see how resourceful you are, and understand through your own work how large your life can be. Your Retrospective is part of your launch pad that will help you rocket out of the world you are in and into the next.

You will use the Retrospective and its accompanying Characteristics exploration again and again throughout the Live Large process. In Chapter 5, you will use them when you are discovering your values and what's important to you. In Chapters 6 and 7, you will find them useful when you are discovering vows you may have made to yourself that are limiting you, or when you are stuck in paradigms that hold you back.

Exploration: Building a Retrospective

In the grid on pg.24, divide your life into three- to five-year segments in the narrow band labeled "ages." Use your age or the year, it doesn't matter which. You'll start with your junior high or high school years, then college years, then move continuing on from there, 22–25, 26–29, and so on. What's fun about this Retrospective is that it encourages you to look forward by imagining the kinds of things you will enjoy doing in the future.

- **Positives**: List the things you loved under each age range. Maybe you were into pickup basketball or reading. What was your favorite subject in school? Were you a social butterfly, always eager to make new friends? What made you smile?

- **Negatives**: Next, list the things you found discouraging or frustrating under each age range. Perhaps you felt left out or had to move frequently. Did you dread going to math class or have a troubling parent or sibling relationship at home? Did you hate your first nine-to-five job?

- **Beliefs about Myself**: Finally, list what you believed about yourself under each age range. What were the qualities or characteristics you felt defined you as a person at the time? Were you great at sports, horrible at math, a great people person, an introvert, not cut out for city life, a homebody, an artist, a failed creative?

- **Recurring Themes**: Look carefully at the three boxes you filled in. Are there words that show up in more than one place? Are there recurring situations you experienced as positive or negative? This could include meeting new people, organizing projects, persuading parents, dealing with bosses, or learning new information. Circle these and then note them in this box. It doesn't matter whether they are negative or positive. These are clues to help you figure out where to go next.

- **Notes to Self**: After you've completed these boxes, are there things you realize or insights you have? Perhaps you see now that you were better at something than you thought you were, or that a lack of preparation has contributed to some failures. Maybe you have gotten back more than what you put in to people or organizations. Write these reflections down here.

> Remember, you can download copies of the Explorations at www.elizabethbcrook.com/explorations.

Your completed Retrospective is full of characteristics that give you insights into who you are—or, perhaps, who you *think* you are. Characteristics are traits, qualities, ways of being, words, or phrases you use to describe yourself or that others may use to describe you: curious, cautious, adventurous, timid, outgoing. Studies suggest that some characteristics are inborn while others are adaptive responses to circumstances. For instance, if you

	Ages 14-17	Ages 18-21	Ages 22-25
Positives Easy Felt good Made me smile Satisfying	• Going away to school • Learning new things, meeting new people from different backgrounds • Going out in the big city • Feeling independent • Glee Club, Literary Club, sports • Travels with my family • Getting really good grades	• Relationships with some professors • A serious boyfriend • Learning new things—really digging in • Fun in the dorm and playing bridge • Summer school • More time in NYC	• Feeling like I was part of NYC and its buzz • Having a job in advertising • Inviting people over to our apartment • Getting married • Public speaking • Organizing projects
Negatives Hard Frustrating Discouraging Scary	• Socially insecure at times • Feeling like others were "in" • Advanced Math—trig and calculus • Having my boyfriend stolen by a friend	• Getting good grades in subjects I didn't enjoy—Physics! • Feeling pulled between being "just a happy freshman/sophomore" and my older boyfriend who made fun of college enthusiasm • Struggled with the line between "being good" and being sophisticated • I wanted to be both apart and "a part" • Feeling like I had different identities	• Getting married • Dealing with how expensive it was to live in NYC • Realizing how much my husband drank every day
Beliefs about Myself	If I work hard, I will be rewarded	I needed to finish college before I could begin "living my life"	If I kept doing the right things, my life would work out
Recurring Themes	I have believed I needed others to keep me safe: the right husband, the right partner, the right advisor		
Notes to Self	I believed until my late forties that my life would work out well if I "kept turning in my homework." I thought that my success depended on someone successful recognizing my work/worth. I realize that I have most of my own good answers, and that I don't have to trade freedom for security.		

	Ages:	Ages:	Ages:
Positives Easy Felt good Made me smile Satisfying			
Negatives Hard Frustrating Discouraging Scary			
Beliefs about Myself			
Recurring Themes			
Notes to Self			

are the independent type, the trait of independence might have shown up naturally as early as your school years. Alternately, you might have learned to be independent because your mom and dad weren't around much.

When we move through our mundane, routine lives, it can be easy to forget that we possess traits that are truly admirable—hero traits, you could call them. Some of our traits may be wildly contradictory—and that's great! It proves our amazing complexity as humans. In the next exploration, you will dive deeper into your characteristics, because if you are trying to move toward living larger, you first need to realize how big you are already. Think of this exploration as a first step toward seeing that "bigness" more clearly.

Exploration: Listing Your Characteristics

Look at the "Recurring Themes" box on your Retrospective. What characteristics do these themes suggest you have? Are you the person who always comes up with new ideas, a visionary, an adventurer, an innovator? Maybe you are easily bored and hard to please. Are you the person who makes sure all steps are followed? Are you diligent, organized, and responsible, or are you rigid and intolerant?

What you are doing in this exploration is creating a picture of yourself. The list of possible characteristics is endless. Here are just a few:

My Characteristics		
Loyal	Big-picture thinker	Connecter
Hardworking	Adventurous	People-oriented
Impatient	Bold	Leader
Love to learn	Resilient	Empathetic
Organized	Independent	Outgoing
Smart	Curious	Shy

My Characteristics		

Write out as many as you like. Go for two dozen! Don't be afraid to list characteristics that seem like opposites. You may be fiercely independent *and* seek reassurance and recognition. You may be impatient with yourself *and* overly patient with people who don't follow through. Again, this simply shows your complexity. Have fun getting to know yourself in this way! When you're finished, draw a circle around the characteristics you think are most responsible for the successes you've had to date in your life.

. . .

Whenever I work intensively with clients, I write down on a big piece of paper all the characteristics that emerge as they tell their story. I write as fast as I can, capturing the impressions I have, and as I write I say, "Tell me when I tell the first lie."

Now here is the interesting thing: No one has ever stopped me. And as many times as not, when I turn around, I will see tears in my client's eyes. When I ask, which I sometimes do, what the tears are about, I have heard the following replies:

"I didn't realize how many good things there are about me."

"I never think of myself that way."

"How do you know these things?"

"Are you sure that's really me?"

"I feel a little embarrassed; no one has ever said those things before."

Remember, before I start this exercise, I ask each person to tell me if I misstate my understanding of who they are. Yet, when someone else can help mirror back to them who they really are, they sit in awe, wonder, and recognition: "Yes, that *is* who I am!"

. . .

The Retrospective hones your ability to reflect, which is a big part of the Live Large process. As achievers, we often do not have time to reflect. We may not notice the patterns or systems of belief—good or bad—that we have cultivated throughout our lives. But once we are aware of our strengths and personal resources, we begin to feel more confident about who we are in the world, and this confidence is one of the most important tools toward making the next big step.

CHAPTER 3

The Rock Solid Necessity of Tears and Fears: The Lifeline

In this chapter you will create a map of your life that I like to call the Lifeline. Similar to the explorations in the previous chapter, the Lifeline gives you a chance to reflect on your life up until now, but unlike the Retrospective, this exploration focuses on *external*, rather than *internal*, events. A foundational exploration to the Live Large process, the Lifeline puts who you are in the context of events and experiences and shows your characteristics in action. It helps you recognize the complexity, fluidity, and variability of your life. The Lifeline gives you a chance to celebrate both how far you've come and how you've managed to move through difficult stages. And because of that, it is a tremendous resource.

The Lifeline gives you the confidence you'll need to complete the subsequent explorations in this book. You will be referring to the Lifeline and its components again and again as you discover hidden talents and gifts you didn't know you had, move through Limiting Beliefs, and begin to outline the myriad possibilities for what's next in Section III. It also gives you reassurance that where you are right now is just another stage in your life. You have had many already, and you will have many more.

Completing the Lifeline reminds me of making vegetable soup. It's not hard, but there are a lot of steps: dice the onions, peel the carrots and potatoes, chop the tomatoes, and so on. So take this one step at a time. If you feel overwhelmed, take a break. Remember, this is not a speed test. Here are the steps you'll be taking:

- You will recall events in your life—they don't all have to be big events!

- You will mark which events were high points and which were low points.

- You will identify the turning points in your life.

- You will give a name or title to the time periods between the turning points.

As you move through the exploration and create your Lifeline, you'll have examples at each step. Let's get started!

Lessons from Greeter Falls

On the Cumberland Plateau in Middle Tennessee flows Greeter Falls. This is a favorite summer haunt for me. The cool waters move over limestone and shale laid down eons ago, when this land once sat at the bottom of an inland sea. Today it runs its course through a canyon bordered by mountain laurel. The upper falls are wide, with a ten-foot drop feeding into a flat sheet of rock—the perfect place to feel the waters rush by before they channel into the fifty-foot drop of Lower Greeter and its deep pool below.

I felt called to Greeter one fall day several years ago. Too chilly for swimming or wading, it offered me a solitary place to leave my sadness and refill my spirit. As I started my hike, I was disappointed by the amount of debris that had been brought down by the big rains over the summer. Leaves and branches were scattered everywhere. Pausing to look for the trail, I became aware that my progress would be made in many small steps, each a decision unto itself.

As I climbed, I saw a large, flat rock in the middle of the stream—the perfect place to sit and enjoy the beauty of the water as it gurgled toward the falls. With my goal in view, I started toward it, step by step. I forged my own path. Large, smooth boulders angling down offered no foothold. I didn't know how I would get over to the rock. I grabbed at tree limbs and searched for anything to hold on to. As I precariously made my way closer to the rock, I glanced down to check my footing. I found I was standing on debris, dead branches, and leaves wedged into crevices between the boulders. This debris had become my stepping-stones.

How often I've looked at the mistakes, the hurts and failures in my life, as so much debris cluttering up the landscape and spoiling the view, instead of seeing them as stepping-stones to a higher place!

Exploration: Writing Your Lifeline: Explorations, Turning Points, and Titles

Under each three- to five-year segment in the following Lifeline, write the events that happened during that time in your life. These age ranges or segments can be the same ones you used in your Retrospective. You can write events you are and are not proud of: It's all grist for the mill. Make sure to write down events you hope will happen in the future. This is often the best part.

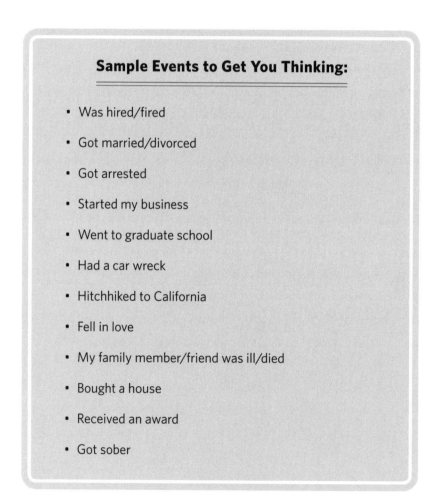

Sample Events to Get You Thinking:

- Was hired/fired

- Got married/divorced

- Got arrested

- Started my business

- Went to graduate school

- Had a car wreck

- Hitchhiked to California

- Fell in love

- My family member/friend was ill/died

- Bought a house

- Received an award

- Got sober

- Started a band

- Got/lost a big account

- Became a parent

If you are writing down events that felt a little like hell at the time, don't forget you wouldn't be who you are now (committed to finding the *what's next* in your life) if you hadn't had these experiences. When my dear friend Yvonne was recording the events in her Lifeline, she had to remember a particularly low period in her life, during which she experienced plenty of rage, tears, and fears. In high school, her son Charlie became angry, sullen, and self-destructive. Although a bright boy, his grades had dropped dramatically. In spite of working with a local counselor, Charlie's behavior did not improve, and Yvonne and her husband were at odds about what to do. Afraid for his safety and as a last resort, they enrolled him in a therapeutic school for kids with behavior issues. These difficulties, combined with her husband's failing business, led to the end of Yvonne's twenty-year marriage.

Completing the Lifeline brought up some of that painful carnage. But it also reminded her of a call with her son's counselor, Keith, which happened after Charlie had returned home full of optimism and ready to start college. Keith had called Yvonne to see how things were going, and Yvonne was delighted to report how well Charlie was doing and how close she and her son had become. Yet even in her happiness for their current situation, she felt heavy and sad for the difficult times they had gone through. When she mentioned that sadness and regret to Keith, he said, "Yvonne, when you look at your son now, what do you see?" All at once, she felt deep gratitude for who her son had become and for their relationship. When she told this to Keith, he said, "That's right, Charlie couldn't be who he is now, and you couldn't be where you are now, if you had skipped a single step."

We all have events in our lives we wish we could forget. But they happened, and the more willing we are to shine a light on them, the less negative impact they will have.

Periods				
Age				
Events				

Chart adapted by permission from the Institute of Cultural Affairs

Once you've filled in your Lifeline with events, review them. This is the map you will use to explore the vast territory of the self, which holds more gifts and strengths than you could ever imagine.

Marking Your High Points, Low Points, and Turning Points

Which of your listed events were high points? Mark those with a ★. Which were low points? Mark those with a ✓. As you look at the highs and lows, what do you notice? Sometimes the highs and lows seem to come in spurts, and sometimes they come all at once. You may also notice that some highs and lows were more than just a high or a low. These standouts mark a turning point: a time when your life began to move in a new direction.

Turning points can answer that old question: "How did I get here?" Your turning points may have occurred after big events: moving across the country, having an affair, going to graduate school, or having breast cancer. Not all big events are turning points, and your turning points are not always big events. Sometimes it's the little things that cause the biggest shifts.

It's not always evident at the time that a turning point is happening, which is why it's so helpful to look back at your Lifeline to identify them. You may have gone to graduate school, but it could be four years before you realize that you are in the wrong field. You could have been arrested three times before you quit drinking or divorced twice before you decided you wanted a different kind of partner. Acknowledging your turning points can help you clarify the pattern and flow of how you got to where you are right now.

Now draw a vertical line to represent the year or age you were when each turning point occurred, re-dividing your Lifeline into periods that may or may not correspond to the three- to five-year segments. Some of these time periods may be very short, and others may be long.

Here's what your Lifeline may look like now:

Periods				
Age	Ages 14–18	Ages 19–23	Ages 24–28	Ages 29–33
Events	• Start high school ★ First girlfriend • Honors student • Get first job at fast-food restaurant ★ Buy first car ★ Spend summer of junior year in Germany on exchange program ★ Graduate high school with honors ★ Go to UC Berkeley	• New friends, new ideas • Stepping out of comfort zone • Being more adventurous ✓ Grades are suffering ★ Meet Rachel • Graduate • Stay in California	• Enjoy life—take it easy • Work in coffee shop • Send out resumes ✓ Job interviews at second/third choice places • Not much available ✓ Break up with Rachel	★ Do independent research for energy and climate program ★ Go back to UCB for master's degree • Back on track ★ Meet Kate— Engaged a year later ★ High Points ✓ Low Points

Identifying your turning points will help you to better understand the turning point you are at right now in your life. If you
were not at a major turning point, you would not have bought
this book. Although our turning points can be the consequence of
trying times or situations, you can tell from your chart that each
represents a doorway to the next best thing. With each new turning point, you are flinging open a door to a much wider horizon.

Titling Your Lifeline

Now that you have used the turning points to create periods of your life, you are going to give a title to each period. These titles will enable you to capture the essence of each period so you can celebrate, honor, and come to peace with them. This is an opportunity to look at the themes of your life across time and to acknowledge that some parts were hard, messy, or filled with self-doubt. Other times, you were riding high. Essentially, this step helps you see that you have always been moving forward. You never have to define yourself by one period of your life.

Beginning with the earliest segment between the first two turning points, ask yourself: "What defined this time for me?" Jot down words or phrases in the space above the events. Whether it is poetic or descriptive, your title should sum up what your life was about during those years. Here are a few examples:

- "The Lost Years"
- "Hell and High Water"
- "On the Launch Pad"
- "Growing Up AGAIN"

Don't forget to name the future period, too! What do you want the next stage of your life to be called?

Here is an example of what your lifeline may look like now:

Periods	**Growing Up** Lots of firsts	**Becoming Independent**	**College Years** Learning, experimenting, changing	**Confused, lacking direction** Graduate from college, relax, hard to get a job in my field, feeling inadequate, a failure	**Realignment** Self-realization, getting focused, master's degree, Becoming me, self-satisfaction
Age	Ages 14-18		Ages 19-23	Ages 24-28	Ages 29-33
Events	• Start high school ★ First girlfriend • Honors student • Get first job at fast-food restaurant ★ Buy first car ★ Spend summer of junior year in Germany on exchange program ★ Graduate high school with honors ★ Go to UC Berkeley		• New friends, new ideas • Stepping out of comfort zone • Being more adventurous ✓ Grades are suffering ★ Meet Rachel • Graduate • Stay in California	• Enjoy life—take it easy • Work in coffee shop • Send out resumes ✓ Job interviews at second/third choice places • Not much available ✓ Break up with Rachel	★ Do independent research for energy and climate program ★ Go back to UCB for master's degree • Back on track ★ Meet Kate— Engaged a year later ★ High Points ✓ Low Points

With your Lifeline completed, take a few minutes to look at and appreciate your full, rich, complex life. Now jot down any thoughts, advice to yourself, or anything else you want to remember about who you really are moving forward.

Notes to Self:

• • •

The Lifeline alone can kick-start all sorts of events. It may help to reignite an idea you had when you were younger that got lost in the daily grind of buying houses, raising kids, caring for an ill relative, or providing for a family. You may realize you finally want to start that business, write a book, or travel around the world. There are endless possibilities that the Lifeline will help you begin to imagine and bring to life.

CHAPTER 4

The Big Why

For almost twenty years, I've been going to the Nashville Women's Breakfast Club, where fifty successful women meet every Wednesday morning to hear a speaker. On the first Wednesday of the month, we also share what's going on in our lives, both personally and professionally. One week I listened as each of these talented, successful women shared her reflections. A retired CEO was finding significance and purpose in her writing. The head of an internationally recognized museum was taking time to go back and read the books we were supposed to read in high school. A well-respected nutrition consultant wanted to work as part of a team and had started talking to companies that might benefit from a CNO (chief nutrition officer). The next-to-last woman to speak, a noted gynecologist who had been practicing for twenty-five years, took a big breath as she stood up. "I'm getting tired," she said. "I want to retire, not to another career, but to *no* career. I don't want to have to do anything but read and take walks and develop some of my hobbies. If I never hear someone ask another question about her uterus again, that would be just fine."

Her comments were met with nervous laughter, and as I looked around the room I observed expressions of both recognition and fear. It was completely natural for this hardworking doctor to have these feelings. However, we are often afraid to admit similar feelings to ourselves, because we fear that we will never again be able to feel enthusiastic about our work.

In fact, feeling worn out and disconnected is a sure sign that you are nearing a turning point. In order to know what direction to take, you must not be afraid to admit those feelings to yourself and reflect upon why you decided to do the work in the first place. What did you want? What was your purpose?

When I work with individuals, one of the first things we do after completing the Lifeline is to find the Why of their lives. The Why is what makes your heart sing. It is your life's overarching theme. I could have made up all sorts of things about what the gynecologist's Why might be, but like you, she is the only one who knows. Perhaps she was one of only a few women in her field when she started practicing medicine, so her Why was to break down barriers and clear the way for others. Or perhaps it was about supporting women to take charge of their own lives. All we know for sure is that at this point in her life, her job no longer satisfies her. To discover happiness again, she must first find her Why. This is true for you as well, whether you are working on your own or whether you founded a huge company and are serving thousands or even millions.

Betty Nixon, a remarkable woman and a true pioneer, ran for mayor of Nashville some twenty years ago. After she retired from a leadership position in community relations and policy at Vanderbilt University, she engaged in writing and speaking engagements to inform others about legislation that would affect their communities. Her Why shone through her work and her life: to give others a voice in those areas that affect their lives and communities. Betty died in August 2016, and was honored in many places for the contributions she made to the community.

Julia retired from modeling in Milan and started a company that created a market for an amazing furniture maker who lived on the coast of Italy. She didn't necessarily want to shift careers, but she had ceased feeling the joy she once did and wanted to feel excited about the work again. She loved design, but she was no longer pursuing this interest. She needed to rediscover her Why. It turned out to be: bringing beauty to the world through artistic collaboration. She now focuses less on marketing and is going back to Italy to develop new designs for the company. Her face lights up when she talks about her new creations. She is also helping the company expand its production and is training young people in what might have been a dying art.

Samuel has been extraordinarily successful. He has grown and sold two companies and frankly could sit on a yacht watching the clouds go by if he chose to. But he doesn't. With no business to run, he began struggling to identify a new center for his life. After all, there were so many things he *could* do, but he didn't know what would connect with both his head and his heart. What Samuel discovered is that he liked to change things—not for the sake of change, but to make things better. He has always been a problem solver. But more than that, he's able to synthesize or bring together disparate ideas and information. It has given him deep satisfaction. So I helped him write out his Why: to facilitate positive change through values-based problem solving and synthesizing results. Now he's exploring different areas and trusts that something will emerge that will align his purpose with his gifts and talents.

The importance of finding the "Why" is also illustrated in the business world. When doing strategic planning with CEOs and entrepreneurs, the first thing I ask them is: "Why does your business exist?" It's never just about the money. Both Village Real Estate and Core Development in Nashville have been a force in keeping Nashville's existing neighborhoods vital and in anchoring some neighborhoods that had seen hard times. Why? Because they believe real estate is a force for positive social and community change.

Another example is Lodge Manufacturing Co, a 120+-year-old company in South Pittsburg, Tennessee, that makes arguably the best cast-iron cookware in the world. You might find a black cast-iron Lodge skillet in your kitchen that came from your great-grandmother or a Lodge Dutch oven your grandfather once used on camping trips. Lodge's Why? Continuing a family tradition and providing products to others so they, too, can continue their own family traditions.

You may be saying: "But my Lifeline proves I've been all over the map—there isn't a single purpose running through it, I have done so much." That's what many people think, but make no mistake: You have one! And, whether you know it or not, you've been living it. Your purpose does not have to be grand or formal sounding, although it might be. The clearer you are about it, the more creative—even wild—you can get about what you do. If you've never had a written purpose before, now is the time to try to tease it out! I know it may feel big, but this isn't set in stone. This is just a step on the road toward discovering what's next in your life.

Exploration: Finding Your Why

I've used this exploration myself, and so have many others. You may want to talk this through out loud with yourself or a trusted friend (think of them as a mirror). There is a power in saying things out loud!

In the chart on pg.48, in the What I Did section, make a list of five to seven jobs you have had that satisfied you in some elemental way. These can be paid and nonpaid positions. For instance, at one point I volunteered with the YWCA to help women learn to be safe and self-sufficient so they could care for themselves and their families. Now I help individuals and organizations see things from a fresh perspective so they have more choices; can do what they do in better, smarter ways; and can fulfill their purpose. Did I know when I was a twenty-something that helping out at the YWCA would grow to become such a big part of my Why? No, but it makes perfect sense in retrospect.

You don't have to list every single position you've held, just jot down the ones you felt most excited and passionate about. For example: an attorney who seeks justice for victims of crime; a guidance counselor assisting students in preparing for the outside world; a PR professional helping companies tell their unique stories; a software developer who creates systems/models that support a fair and just world; a financial advisor enabling clients to feel empowered about their money; even a summer job that felt important: a sales rep for Clinique who helped women feel beautiful. Nothing is off the table!

Now fill in the Why column. What seemed to be your driving force in doing this work? Why were you doing what you were doing? Do the themes of your Whys relate to one another? Are you starting to see an overall purpose?

Remember: Your Why does not have to be grand and formal sounding. It just needs to feel right. Because once you know your purpose, there are many, many ways to fulfill it.

What I did	Why I did it/ why it mattered
Selling information to business	It helped them sell their products and be more successful in their business
Family planning education	It gave people more control of their lives
Raising money for literacy	People who read have more opportunity for themselves and their family
Cross-cultural training	When people learn to function in another culture they are able to do more and be happier
Organization development	Skilled management gets the best performance from employees and people feel better about the place they work
System development and computer training	Using technology lets people do their work faster and smarter
Business consulting	Helping entrepreneurs grow helps their employees and their communities

Purpose: Help individuals and organizations do what they do in a better, smarter way—to see things from a fresh perspective and have more choices and yes, fulfill their purpose.

Again if your Why doesn't pop out for you, don't be discouraged. Heidi Hartman, the Momentum Manager for my company, Orchard Advisors, and one of the most energetic and determined people I know, told me she had trouble with this. "All I could come up with," she said, "was service, learning, and connection."

But what a beautiful purpose statement those three words can create! Each represents a compelling theme all its own. Such a statement could be written several ways:

- "I serve others through connection and increase my capacity to do so through learning."

- "I serve by connecting people and helping others learn about themselves and each other."

- "I connect with others to learn how to best be of service."

Only Heidi can know where she wants the emphasis to be. And guess what? She doesn't have to decide. She is already clear that her purpose, her calling in life, is to serve, connect, and learn. It can be as simple and as profound as that.

What I did	Why I did it/ why it mattered

Purpose:

• • •

Throughout the Live Large journey, you will be using your Why to focus yourself back toward what you do. There are a lot of moving parts to finding out what's next, and your Why is one of those bedrock elements you can lean on moving forward. Instead of asking yourself, "Is this the right thing?" you can ask, "Does it fit my Why?" If yes, then you are on the right track. We will be using it to great effect in Section III, when we begin to put the pieces together to find the Bull's-eye of what you want to achieve. The Why is instrumental in helping you outline the pragmatic possibilities available at your fingertips.

How do you know for sure you have just discovered your Why? It will feel familiar. It's like running into a dear friend you haven't thought of in a while. It makes you want to smack your head and say, "Of course! Of course this is my purpose. I sort of knew this, but I had forgotten." You may have a similar experience in the next chapter, when you begin to articulate your values.

CHAPTER 5

Finding Values in a Latin American Disco

When I moved to Venezuela in my thirties, I could only speak basic Spanish. I could count to ten and say "please," "thank you," and "milk." Eventually I learned the language and was hired by a privately funded national literacy program. Part of my job was to convince national and multinational organizations to get involved with our program by sponsoring literacy programs in their factories and raising money for the hundreds of literacy groups in rural Venezuela, where there were no factories. I traveled to rural areas often, sometimes by car, sometimes in the back of a National Guard truck. I ate *arepas* while sitting on the dirt floor of mountain huts with potato farmers, and hen stew on the fly-covered back porch of a chicken farmer. I was thrilled to be there—not just because it was my first real job speaking Spanish, but also because I was getting paid to do something I felt was congruent with my values. The work satisfied my Why to "make the world a better place."

The inefficiencies in the operation were challenging, but I chalked it up to being a "start-up." All was well until Secretary's Day, a big celebration in Caracas, when my general manager told us we would be closing the office at midday for lunch to celebrate. I walked out of the sunny Caracas day into a cool nightclub, where I found a table laid out for the entire organization with bottles of aged whiskey running down the middle. Gold metallic palm trees ringed the dance floor, and colored lights flashed in rhythm with the disco music. I had asked our donors to fund literacy programs, and here I was in a nightclub with a state-of-the-art sound system. All I could think of was: "Who is paying for this?" Of course I knew the answer, which led to my next thought: "I hope none of our funders learn about it!"

Frankly, I can barely remember the rest of the afternoon, and it wasn't from drinking Scotch. I was floored that we could be asking corporations for financial support while we were spending money on boozing it up at a nightclub in the middle of the day. Once I thought about it, other "inappropriate expenditures" seemed to strongly violate our fiduciary responsibility to our donors. I didn't have the words those many years ago to talk about a clash of values, but I knew I could not stay.

Working in a job that asks you to do things that are against your values is not healthy. And in the end, leaving was the best thing I ever did. I found another job in the private sector that turned out to be the beginning of a whole new career, and which helped me plant the seeds for what I do today.

When you identify your values, you make explicit something that is already true about you. Your values can guide your actions and keep you connected to the world. They allow you to live with depth, purpose, and authenticity—and that is what Living Large is all about.

Our values are so intrinsic to who we are that many times they live outside our awareness. Because of this, it can be hard to put our finger on that feeling that something isn't right. If you spend some time considering your values, you will be able to face that feeling more directly by asking: "Am I being called on to act counter to what's most important to me?" In other words, knowing our values can help us make the hard call.

Values are your best characteristics in action. Identifying how you act when you feel good about yourself is key to understanding your core values and living in a way that makes you satisfied on a deep level. Refer to the exploration of your Characteristics in Chapter 2. Which ones point to who you are when you are at your best? "Persistent." "Loyal." "Hardworking." Star these characteristics. In a perfect world we are acting out our best characteristics or otherwise behaving in a way that's congruent with them.

Exploration: Discovering Your Values

In the following chart, list times or situations when you felt proud of yourself. Then in the space beside, write a statement that reflects a value you hold. Here are some examples:

When I felt proud/ good about myself	The value I was living
I took care of my mother through her illness	I am compassionate and loving
I finally stopped being angry at someone who had wronged me	I am willing to forgive—consider others' feelings
After my house burned down, I started a gratitude journal	I am grateful, show gratitude
When Google Docs altered my manuscript I reconsidered some of the text and sequencing	I am resilient—when things go wrong, keep trying
I handled my parents' estate fairly	I am a person of integrity

When I felt proud/ good about myself	The value I was living

If this exploration feels challenging, you might try asking a couple of people who know you well to describe what you're doing when you are being your best self. This will give you hints. Or at the end of a day or a situation that you felt good about, ask yourself how you "showed up." Fill in the blank: *I am/acted/showed . . .*

• • •

By understanding where you have been, your values, and your purpose, you have built a launch pad for Living Large. You will be referencing these again and again as you step toward discovering a richer, more intentional life. Now that you have discovered or rediscovered what makes you the unique person you are, the world is your oyster. Unfortunately, it's not always that simple. Some things may still hold us back from what we imagine or dream we could have, be, and accomplish. I call these your Limiting Beliefs. In the next section you will identify these beliefs and understand how they work so you can break free of their power to get in your way. You will also explore the incredible and singular talent hiding in the Retrospective and the Lifeline you just completed.

SECTION

Breaking Through Your Bonds and the Diamonds in Your Own Backyard

"Know thyself."
—Socrates

"We run away all the time to avoid coming face-to-face with ourselves."
—Author Unknown

"We have met the enemy, and he is us."
—Pogo (cartoon character)

"Failure is simply the opportunity to begin again more intelligently."
—Henry Ford

CHAPTER 6

Missing the Magic Show: What Kinds of Beliefs Hold Us Back

O ne of the most important and surprising things we can do when we want to Live Large is to take a really close look at our personal beliefs. Beliefs are something you hold to be true, whether they are or not. They are an invisible set of rules that have the power to limit what we can imagine, think, or do. Beliefs can contribute to negative self-talk (the Triple J) and self-defeating actions. But when we see our beliefs clearly, we are able to make choices based on clarity.

Beliefs turn into vows when we experience something emotional or even traumatic and our sense of risk is great. A vow is a hyperbolized belief, a promise to yourself, a declaration. We often know we've made a vow when *always* and *never* turn up in a statement about what we believe. "I will *never* make that mistake again!"

When I was six, my father was going to take me to a magic show in a downtown hotel. You can imagine my excitement. Since my grandmother lived in an apartment in the hotel, my mother took me there to dress before he picked me up. At six I was a dawdler. I couldn't seem to do anything fast. I was frequently distracted, and in spite of my mother's urging, I didn't get dressed. When my father arrived, I was not ready. So, he left. The tears and floor-pounding went on until I was totally exhausted. I couldn't believe he had left me.

Of course I was too young to make a conscious vow, but my mother would always say, "Ever since that day her father left her, Elizabeth has never been late." Years later, I found myself experiencing anxiety about being late for anything, even when it didn't matter. How much sense did that make? Not much, especially when I lived in Latin America where to come "on time" was practically considered rude!

Vows and beliefs come in all different (sneaky) packages. Understanding the potent ways they show up can help you identify when you have made one. Below are the three different types of vows and beliefs that may be sabotaging you.

1. **Vows or beliefs that were true once upon a time:**

    - My mother told me when I was a child that I was selfish, so I must be selfish.

    - When I was a teen I felt unattractive, so now I can't believe the praise or compliments from others.

    - My alcoholic father made our home unpredictable, so now I need to control my situation no matter what.

All that may be true: When you were four, you didn't want to share your toys. As a teen you felt unattractive, and the braces and pimples didn't help. It *was* scary having an unpredictable alcoholic at home, and that made it feel safer to control as much as you could. But circumstances change and once-upon-a-time beliefs like these become irrelevant—yet they still manage to rule our lives.

2. **Beliefs that were never true:**

For centuries, people believed the Earth was the center of the universe and that the sun revolved around it. This was a belief that was never true. Just because learned scholars believed it still didn't make it so. Your parents probably told you that Santa could see if you were naughty or nice. Just because we believed doesn't mean this was *ever* true! What we call "old wives' tales" (don't go out in the cold after a hot shower . . .) provide other examples of beliefs that were never true. Of course, a favorite example is civilization's belief that the world was flat and if you sailed west from Europe, you would drop off the side. It's good to remember that it was only when that belief was challenged and discarded that real exploration for a new world began.

3. **Beliefs that were true for someone else but not true for you:**

Once upon a time, a husband noticed that when his wife cooked a roast she cut the ends off. When he asked her why, she said that was the way her mother did it. Curious, the young husband asked his mother-in-law why *she* cut the ends off the roast. The mother-in-law replied that *her* mother always cooked her roast that way. They both believed this was *the* way to cook a roast.

A few weeks later, the young man told his wife's grandmother about the conversations and asked the older woman why she cut the ends off the roast. She laughed and said, "I don't know why *they* cut the ends off their roasts, but I just never had a pan big enough." It's so easy to do something simply because it's always been done that way. That roast in the pan is a small example, but it represents much bigger beliefs in our lives that we haven't thought to question. When a belief we hold was true at some time for someone else, but not for us, that belief can cripple us physically, intellectually, and emotionally.

• • •

Now that you can see some beliefs were never true, no longer true, or not true for you, you may notice how they tend to manage your life, keeping you stuck in patterns that resemble the looped track on a treadmill. The good news? Just reading about them can trigger insights about what may be holding you back. If you can name your particular Limiting Beliefs (we all have them, so it's nothing to be ashamed of!), you can move forward into the larger life that's waiting for you. This is some of the most powerful, life-changing work you will do in the book. As you move ahead into the explanations of how Limiting Beliefs show up and the explorations that follow, take them at your own pace. Do what makes sense for you, and remember: If you show up, you can't fail.

CHAPTER 7

Softy/Hard-Ass, Lady Peas, and Other Stubborn Dichotomies

Have you ever made a vow that is limiting what you truly want in your life? Are there beliefs that are limiting you right now? One sure way to identify these limitations we place on ourselves is by paying attention to the following:

- When you use the words always/never

- When you feel like you are stuck in either/or—feeling damned if you do and damned if you don't

- When what you are doing isn't giving you the results you want

- When the same situation keeps happening over and over and you can't seem to stop it

Our mission in this chapter is to identify the everyday beliefs that are working (right now!) to limit your possibilities.

A bright, intense entrepreneur named Sean came to me because he was in a business relationship that wasn't paying off. As we talked, he revealed this wasn't the first business that hadn't worked out. "I'm an outsider type," he told me. "I tend to pick others like me. I feel more comfortable that way. Frankly I've *never* trusted people who seemed like they were part of the 'in-crowd.' And it really makes me mad when I see other people without my smarts get ahead. I can't figure it out."

Sean was an innovator. He had created a new technology to revolutionize his industry. But he wasn't a connector or a promoter. Because he didn't trust "those types," his ideas had never taken hold. He had no one to help get them out into the world. When I asked him how long he'd felt that way, he said, "I've *always* felt that way. My father was in business with some big shots and he got totally screwed. I *never* wanted that to happen to me."

By now, you can fill in the blanks of Sean's story. He vowed *never* to be like his father, *never* to get screwed by big shots, *never* to get involved with "insiders." Holding on to this vow assured Sean he was unlikely to ever connect with the people who could actually help him bring his ideas to fruition. His belief that getting involved with "big shots" was risky had been true for his father, but it prevented Sean from getting what he truly wanted. He'd set himself up for failure *and* for feeling screwed by the big shots, who he believed got attention for ideas that were inferior to his.

Recognizing when we attach "always" and "never" to our beliefs can be the key to knowing if a belief has turned into a vow. "I've NEVER been good at math" is different from "I'm not as good in math as my brother, who is a physicist."

One of my values is extending hospitality. I value being gracious and creating an environment where my guests are comfortable and can enjoy themselves. In order to live these values, I *believed* that when I entertained, I *always* had to make things close to perfect and *never* ask for help. There was nothing wrong with the value of being gracious and making my guests comfortable until I believed I always had to make entertaining perfect and do it all by myself every single time. I could easily turn a simple dinner with friends into a stressful evening, losing sight of the real purpose: to create a welcoming environment for people I care about.

If you can only be one way, you're sure to encounter situations in which that way simply doesn't work. A broken watch is right twice a day but wrong the rest of the time. You wouldn't wear a bathing suit in frigid weather or a parka in the summer. So it is with anything you do, and the danger with *always* and *never* is that they can turn strengths into liabilities.

Either/Or

The either/or trap can come alive in any aspect of our lives, and can hamper our ability to act effectively. Either/or thinking defines situations as either black or white, eliminating any gray, pink, or purple.

My friend Eric is the oldest of three boys. Growing up, he was continually encouraged to share his toys and games with his brothers. Anything else would be considered selfish and "bad." All the boys are grown now and have children of their own, but one of Eric's brothers frequently wants to borrow things or be catered to. The other night when we were out to dinner, he confessed (with some embarrassment) that sometimes he just wants to say no, but he feels guilty. Yet when he talked about some of his brother's requests, I realized Eric was having trouble discerning what was a reasonable request and what wasn't . . . and believe me, some of his brother's requests were over the top. In his mind, he either has to give it all away or he's selfish.

The worst part of the either/or trap is that it feels bad no matter what we do. Eric hated feeling taken advantage of by his brothers, but that seemed better than "acting bad," which is how he defined putting limits on his brothers' demands. Thus, he put himself in an either/or bind in his relationships with them. This bind can be incredibly limiting, especially when it is based on an old belief that we formed as a child.

The story of Sharon offers us another example of the limiting effects of the either/or dichotomy. Before becoming a successful entrepreneur, Sharon had been employed by a company that couldn't deliver the high-quality products and services she was able to sell. She reasoned that if a company with poor service could be in business, imagine what a company with great service could do! So she started her own company in the basement of her house. Now, she has a full manufacturing facility that is growing rapidly and will be a hundred-million-dollar company within the next five years.

When we met, she wanted to talk about one of her senior employees. He had made mistakes that cost the company over one hundred thousand dollars and had acted in other ways that were troubling. She described a number of situations where he had acted contrary to her direction in dealing with staff and vendors. "But he's smart and a valuable employee. He's young, and I wonder if this is just bad judgment on his part. Should I just let it go? I don't want to be too harsh, but it doesn't seem right."

It's important to know that Sharon is a tough cookie. She knows her business inside out and negotiates prices to the penny. She's a straight shooter and doesn't mess around. Because of her forceful manner, you would never think of her as being a softy. But in this situation, that's exactly what she was being, and it didn't feel good. The fact is Sharon, like Eric, was caught in the trap of either/or thinking.

I drew the following diagram for her:

Either/Or
Softy/Hard-ass

"Your challenge is that when you hold your employee accountable, you perceive yourself as being a real hard-ass," I explained.

"That is totally what I do," she told me.

"It sounds like, even though you don't want to be taken advantage of, the thing you most want to avoid is being unfairly critical or demanding. Was there someone when you were growing up who was a real hard-ass, that made you want to be anything *but* that?"

She smiled in recognition. "Yes: my father. He was a real dictator, and I do whatever I can to not be like him!"

It makes perfect sense that Sharon would stay stuck being a softy even when a stronger style would be more appropriate. The only way she can guarantee that she won't be a hard-ass (and thus "bad," like her father) is to be a softy. If you believe there are only two options, softy and hard-ass (either/or), then it feels safer, even if it's uncomfortable, to be a softy than the alternative.

In your head it seems like there are two and only two possibilities:

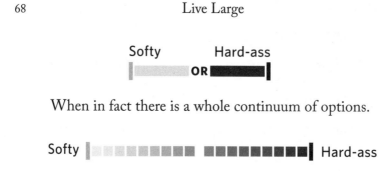

When in fact there is a whole continuum of options.

Below is an image of how Sharon feels when she wants to set limits. She feels as if she is standing on a precipice, and if she takes one step away from being a softy, she will fall into the abyss of bad, or being a hard-ass.

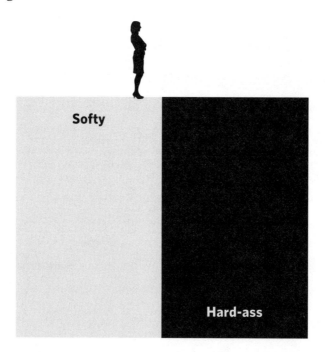

"But how do I change this?" Sharon asked.

So, I told her a story. In the summertime I like to cook big batches of peas: crowder peas, lady peas, purple hull peas, and the like. When I finish cooking and the peas have cooled, I put them in plastic containers, saving them for meals over the next several days. Over a time I noticed that while I selected containers that *looked* like the right size to me, they were invariably several times too big. When my mother came to visit, she said, "I used to do the same thing. Now I pick a container that looks like half the size I need. And guess what? The peas fit perfectly every time!"

We all have areas where our own perceptions are skewed. Once we know what those areas are, we can learn to compensate. In Sharon's case her perception was that there was either one way or the other. As she moves forward, she will have to live with her own discomfort while experimenting with something that doesn't feel quite right. Once she understands she has many options—from very, very softy, to medium soft, to medium hard—she can choose how to respond appropriately.

The story of the peas also illustrates that most of us have a pretty good sense or instinct about what's called for, what's appropriate, and what's reasonable, and we can operate on automatic pilot. Yet we all have one or two areas where the gut is wrong—the blind spots. That's when we need to shift from automatic pilot to manual control, recognizing that our "gut" in those particular situations is not reliable, because earlier experiences have established "rules" about what we can and should do.

When the gut is wrong, we have an opportunity to:

1. Be self-aware.

2. Override our instincts in those areas where our instincts have proved to be unreliable.

Even with an understanding about the either/or dilemma and her reluctance to be a hard-ass, Sharon may always feel a cringe of discomfort when she's holding people accountable. This is normal: We all have areas where we are not good at discerning what a balanced approach looks like. Simply recognizing that the either/or paradigm exists is enough to set us free. If we can't see how many options are available to us, our responses will be severely limited.

False Equivalencies

Like always/never and either/or, false equivalencies are sneaky Limiting Beliefs we may be carrying around without realizing it. False equivalencies are defined by the belief that accomplishing or possessing something will bring a specific result, even if it won't, or that doing or not doing something will make us "good" or "bad." Usually, our rational self knows the false equivalency is not true. If someone asks you if money buys happiness or if people with PhDs feel more loved than people with lesser degrees, you would laugh and say, "Of course not!" But inside all of us lie some unexamined equivalencies.

Emma came to a workshop with me looking for what was next in her life and wanting to live larger. She had been in the hospitality industry, profitably managing food operations for a succession of companies. Yet in every conversation, it became apparent that she felt like she couldn't leave her current career. When we did the exercise on overusing a strength, Emma smiled. "I just realized that I have held on to a career I stopped loving a long time ago because I didn't want to be one of those people who gives up. My grandmother used to say, 'Only quitters quit,' and I'm not a quitter.

You can call me anything, but *never* call me a quitter. In my family that was close to a mortal sin! I realize this plays out not just in my career but in my personal life as well. Even though my first marriage was bad, my husband was verbally abusive and didn't help out, I felt like I had to stick with it or I would have been a quitter. That's crazy thinking, isn't it?"

"What do you believe now?" I asked her.

She laughed. "It's so obvious now. Now I realize that leaving my old career or getting out of an abusive marriage is not the same as being a quitter. This is an amazing realization! It reminds me of that Kenny Rogers song 'The Gambler,' with its good advice about when to hold and when to fold. Sometimes it's important to hold on even when it's hard, and sometimes the wisest thing to do is to stop!"

Emma has renewed that teaching certificate she got long ago and is happily working in a grade school walking distance from her house. She loves her "kids" and feels like she is contributing to her community, but she knows if she gets burned out, it's okay to try something else.

● ● ●

When figuring out whether you might be limiting your life with false equivalencies, it can be helpful to look back at the list of Characteristics you made in Section I. We all have characteristics that are good . . . until we overuse them. We overuse them because we are fearful we may become the opposite (if I'm not persistent, I'm a quitter).

The following list is a sample of the types of false equivalencies we create:

- Having money/a degree/good looks/fame = being loved/ safe/respected/in control/worthy/happy

- Tolerating unacceptable conditions = being patient

- Not being persistent = being a quitter

- Taking time off = being lazy

- Wanting to make money = being greedy/selfish

- Aspiring to do more than my parents = being arrogant/ dissatisfied

- Wanting nice things for myself and my family = being shallow/materialistic

Once you become aware of your false equivalencies, it's much easier to ask: "What do I really know to be true?" Like Emma, you may realize that sometimes doing the opposite of your characteristic is, in fact, a strength.

CHAPTER 8

The Vicious Cycle

The reason the dichotomies of always/never, either/or, and false equivalencies are so intractable is that they lead to something called the Vicious Cycle. A Vicious Cycle is when you harbor a Limiting Belief or vow that leads to the same uncomfortable negative thoughts or situations continuing to pop up in your life. For instance:

- I'm the one who always has to do everything.

- I can never catch a break.

- I never seem to have enough money.

- I am forever rushing around at the last minute.

- I'm going to be late . . . again.

- I just can't decide.

- I have to stop this procrastination.

- People get upset when I express my opinion.

A Vicious Cycle leaves you feeling sad, hopeless, frustrated, and complaining about the same sort of situation over and over. The people in our lives react to the cycle and respond in a way that serves to reconfirm our Limiting Belief. We act accordingly, and we stay stuck! Similar to self-fulfilling prophecies, Vicious Cycles can keep us from feeling valued and happy in our lives. Yet when we reverse them, it's incredibly freeing.

A good example of someone in a Vicious Cycle is Lisanne, a native Californian who married early in an effort to escape from a difficult home environment. Her husband was abusive, and in spite of having two young children, she ended the marriage.

When we first met, she was working as the director of business development for a law firm. Originally she'd been hired to help on the administrative side, but as the company grew, she began doing business development: putting together proposals, organizing events, and representing the firm at networking events.

Lisanne loved the firm and loved telling people about the great work they did. But because she wasn't a lawyer, she didn't feel valued. In trying to build herself up to her team members, she would go on about the work she was doing. Over time, people began to tune her out or cut her off. Since Lisanne was sensitive to such slights, she felt even less valued than before.

And—in Lisanne's mind—why should she feel valued in the first place, given her family background and her unhappy marriage? Here was her Vicious Cycle:

* In order to be valued, she talked more about what she did.

* Talking too much caused people to tune her out.

* Being tuned out left her believing she was undervalued.

Because Lisanne's role had evolved, the firm never had any specific budget for the extra projects she was taking on, so she had to ask her boss repeatedly for money. This began to sound like whining. And what do we do with people who whine? We give them even less time and attention. And the less time and attention Lisanne got, the less valued she felt. The more she tried to get recognition, the more strident she became, the less credibility she had, and the more the boss avoided meeting with her.

My Boss Doesn't Seem to Care

I Feel Undervalued, Unappreciated, Unheard

I Feel the Constant Need to Convince My Boss of My Worth

My Boss Gets Tired of Listening and Withdraws

My Insecurity Drives Me to Seek More Recognition

How can this Vicious Cycle be turned into a virtuous one? In this case, I was working with the firm, so I was able to help them intervene in the cycle. First I took a look at Lisanne's beliefs—especially her false equivalencies. Lisanne felt that talking about how much work she did equaled getting recognition for her work, so I asked her if she would be willing to experiment by talking less about what she was doing.

"Then I'll *never* get credit for what I do," she worried.

"Is what you are doing getting the results you want?" I asked her.

"Not really," she reluctantly agreed.

So she went off the autopilot of her Limiting Beliefs and switched to manual control. In her case, that meant talking less and shining the light on her work less. Lisanne's situation didn't change right away, but little by little, as she stopped trying to stay in the spotlight, she found herself answering more questions about her work. People were interested and curious, and that made her feel valuable.

In Lisanne's case, the Vicious Cycle involved her relationship with her boss and coworkers. However, we can set up our own Vicious Cycle all by ourselves! As the famous cartoon character Pogo said, "We have met the enemy, and he is us!"

The Vicious Cycle

It Has Unfavorable
Consequences

I'm Not Good At
Making Decisions

I'm Afraid
to Make the
Wrong Choice

Then I Have to
Make a Snap Decision

I Postpone
or Avoid Them

A few years back my client Jonathan started a security company. His partner focused on developing the new business while Jonathan handled the inside operations. This wasn't Jonathan's first business; he'd also started an urban delivery service just out of college. Cash had been limited, and he knew making one wrong decision could put him out of business. Often, he postponed making decisions until it was too late, and he had to make a snap decision. One of these decisions put him out of business.

In his new venture, he found himself plagued by his fear of making a wrong decision. Again, he postponed decisions until he had to make snap decisions. By the time Jonathan and his partner called me, this had become an issue. We mapped out the Vicious Cycle. I asked him, "Where do you see an opportunity to break the cycle?"

His answer was brilliant. "Since my current way of making decisions [postponing then making snap decisions] is leading to bad decisions, which is my fear, I can start making decisions sooner. Even if I make one that doesn't work out, that's no different than what's happening now!"

"So," I asked, "what would help you make decisions when they first arise?"

"First, just recognizing that I'm getting poor results by postponing! Second, ask myself what are the criteria, the most important things—price, quality, speed, locally available, and so on. Third, what is the essential information I need? Fourth, decide."

Bingo! Jonathan recognized that his fear had led him to act in a way that reinforced his negative belief. With practice, he was less fearful, was able to act with greater confidence, and began making better decisions in a timely way. He got himself out of a high-stakes Vicious Cycle, and you know what? You can too.

Common Examples of
Vicious Cycles

I Don't Have
Enough Money

I Spend Money
Inappropriately

I Can't Do
What I Want

I Need to Do Something
Special to Make
Myself Feel Better

I Feel Sorry
for Myself

I Have Too
Much to Do

No Action Means More
Things Are Piling Up

I Feel Overwhelmed
and Anxious

Indecision Leads
to No Action
(More Anxiety)

Anxiety Leads
to Indecision

What Keeps the Vicious Cycle Going?

The perpetuation of the Vicious Cycle goes back to the power of belief—particularly Limiting Beliefs—and our need to prove those beliefs right, if only to our subconscious. We often make vows to ourselves during emotionally trying times when we are trying to make sense of what is happening. Because of her upbringing, Lisanne didn't believe she had any value, and she kept proving herself right through her actions.

If I believe things are going to be awful because that made sense at an emotionally risky time when I needed *something* to make sense, even if it was a negative something, I'll act accordingly. I will be angry and unhappy, but I will be right! We feel a twisted satisfaction when the things we predict will go wrong, actually go wrong. We want to shout: "See, I was right! The situation sucks, and I was right!" What we fail to consider in these situations is that our own attitude and actions played a big role in things going badly.

You create virtuous cycles by acting as if what you *believed* were true. Here's an example of how it works: If you anticipate people in your new workplace will be friendly, you will likely feel relaxed. Being relaxed, you will be more likely to open up to people, believe in their good intentions, and offer trust. And guess what? People will be more likely to respond to you in a friendly way, regardless of whether they are normally friendly or not. Even when something goes wrong or there is a miscommunication, nobody takes it personally because you've demonstrated the capacity to see the best in people.

The same stability that gets created in a virtuous cycle is one of the reasons it's so hard to break a Vicious Cycle. If you believe you're entering a "dog-eat-dog" competitive workplace, will you be likely to share your ideas and look for ways to collaborate? Probably not. And the more you withhold and protect your ideas, the more others will treat you in the same way, and you will have unintentionally created the very "dog-eat-dog" environment you feared. If someone does offer you a hand, you will be suspicious of her motives, reject her help, and continue with your theory about your workplace. In this situation, everyone loses . . . most of all you.

• • •

Remember, none of these false equivalencies or Vicious Cycles, none of these always/nevers or either/ors mean you are stuck forever. We are all works in progress. Understanding ourselves is not a "one and done" activity. It is a lifelong curiosity and commitment to self-awareness and self-compassion! Even people who have created dream businesses, own islands in the Caribbean, and are living fantastic lives are exploring their Limiting Beliefs all the time so they can grow bigger. This is the ongoing nature of self-exploration. And it is one of the keys to living large.

CHAPTER 9

Raising the Dead

It's not always easy to explore Limiting Beliefs that are keeping you from living large because it's not always easy to find them. From secreted hiding spaces, they whisper directions or commands, telling us how to think, act, or feel, and without even realizing it, they lead to self-defeating behaviors. Beliefs and vows are sneaky, and in order to really suss them out, you have to find those hiding spaces. That's what this chapter is all about.

Identifying where they might be hiding in your life is a central tenet in living a richer, more satisfying life. Limiting Beliefs may be tucked away in your family and cultural background, hiding in the list of characteristics you created, or buried in the turning points you identified in your Lifeline. Bringing these beliefs (and the corresponding behaviors) to light gives you a tremendous amount of power. You get to choose what works for you, rather than allowing the Limiting Beliefs to do the choosing for you.

Generational and/or Cultural Beliefs

My husband's parents grew up under the dictatorship of General Juan Vicente Gómez, a ruthless man who ruled Venezuela from 1908 until his death in 1935. At one point, he was thought to be the wealthiest man in South America, in part because he would demand property: land, animals, and personal possessions. He always demanded the most treasured, prized possessions. It was his way of testing loyalty. In order to defend their families and their fortunes, many Venezuelans became extremely fearful of letting *anyone* know what was important to them, lest Gómez demand they surrender it.

Although General Gómez died in 1935, persisting throughout the culture was a reluctance to let anyone know what they valued. *Be careful. If someone knows you value that horse, you may have to give it up.* You can imagine how difficult it could be in a relationship today if one of the partners still has this belief (*don't let anyone know what you truly prize*). The endurance of family and cultural norms is strong, and we may adhere to them without knowing it. Here are some common generational and cultural beliefs that many people carry around with them. (Remember that sometimes we do the opposite of what we are told, and that means we are still being controlled by the old belief!):

- *Money*: "Hoard your money, or someday you could lose it all." Did a great-grandparent lose everything in the Great Depression?

- *Business*: "People like that always take advantage of people like us." Did a certain class or culture of people take advantage of "your people"?

- *Marriage*: "It's important to stay married for the children." Did your mother or grandmother stay in an unhappy marriage because she thought it would be better for the kids?

Most beliefs that come from your family start with good intentions. Your parents, teachers, or mentors wanted to help by making you stronger, safer, and so on. So rather than place blame, we can become curious about how we hold on to the positive while also not getting trapped by the dangerous dichotomies. Living large means having the freedom to choose and not be manipulated by old, hidden, default reactions.

The central question to ask is this: "What serves me now?" As we move through the next round of explorations, you will find yourself answering this exact question so you can live a life not dictated by any previous limitations.

Exploration: Excavating Generational Beliefs

Filling out the following chart will begin the process of excavating those outdated beliefs that no longer serve you. You may not have strong beliefs on every topic, and that's okay. Like many of the other explorations, you may revisit this chart at any point in the future when you find yourself in a stuck place. Here's an example of some answers you could give:

	My family believes	Positive intention	Possible negative result	What is my enlightened belief? What serves me now?
Money	Money keeps you safe	Make sure you have money to meet your needs and take care of yourself	I save all I can and find it hard to spend on nice things for myself and my family	With my income, I can afford to save <u>and</u> also have enough for my family
Work	If you work hard, you will get ahead. You should never seek recognition for that	Work is an important part of being an adult and there is pleasure in a job well done	I don't worry about office politics because I work hard and never take credit for what I do, so I don't get recognized for the value I bring	I realize that it's OK to seek recognition for the job I've done <u>and</u> take pleasure in a job well done
Happiness	We don't expect to be happy. That's just for fairy tales	We want to protect you from disappointment when things don't work out your way	I put up with intolerable situations because I don't believe I deserve to be happy	I deserve happiness in my life <u>and</u> I understand that sometimes life comes with disappointments
Possessions	When you have expensive things, people will respect you	A good impression may open up doors to opportunity	I buy things I don't need. I always have to buy the "best" or most expensive	My possessions don't define me. They are not why my friends like me or respect me
Relationships				
People who are not like us				
What is worthy				
Whom/ what do you trust?				

Now it's your turn:

	My family believes	Positive intention	Possible negative result	What is my enlightened belief? What serves me now?
Money				
Work				
Happiness				
Possessions				
Relation-ships				
People who are not like us				
What is worthy				
Whom/what do you trust?				

This chart can help you when you move toward any major decision in your life or anytime you feel stuck—for example, not happy at work or in your relationships, upset about money, or unclear about who to trust. It is much easier to find a clear path forward when you know which of the beliefs are yours and which you inherited.

Using Your Characteristics to Discover Your Limiting Beliefs and Vows

When you listed your Characteristics in Section I, you may not have known it, but you already managed the hard work of uncovering your Limiting Beliefs. And it's incredible how many of our strengths, when hyperbolized, can limit us. One of the best examples I've ever seen of this was when Jerry, an engineer in a large automotive plant, came to me for help. He was bright, creative, and could figure out problems that left others stumped. It wasn't long before his boss promoted him to engineering manager, and he became part of the operations team. Although his boss had high expectations, and Jerry was excited about the opportunity, people found him difficult. His boss said if he couldn't learn to get along better with his peers, his career there would be limited.

When I met Jerry, he wanted to make a career out of his work as an engineer. He had big plans for himself in the field and was baffled about the friction he'd encountered on the Plant Operations Team. In order to move him forward, we started with his Retrospective and his Lifeline. While he was making a list of his characteristics, we found that the positive far outweighed the negative.

When I asked Jerry which characteristics he was proudest of, he replied, "I'm proudest that I learned to rely on myself. My father left us alone when I was still a kid. I had to learn to take care of myself. I have been able to go far and get an education, even though we didn't have much money. My greatest strength was learning how to rely on myself."

"How has that played out at work?" I asked him.

"When there are problems on the floor, I just dig in. I don't really ask anyone else for help, I just keep going until I find a solution. The truth is, I think it's a weakness to keep running to someone else to fix your problems."

"And what about now? How do you work with your peers at the plant?" I continued.

"I almost always know what needs to be done, but it seems like people get mad when I come up with a solution. I get impatient when they can't see what I'm saying, and I guess I sometimes come out blasting."

For Jerry, what had been a strength (learning to rely on himself) became counterproductive when it was his only way to respond. If Jerry had been dependent instead of self-reliant as a kid, he would never have had the opportunities he had. But in order to deal with his fear of dependence, he overused his characteristic of self-reliance, and it interfered with his ability to work well with his peers and allow others to contribute to solutions. Through our work together, he learned that "enlightened" self-reliance left space to work with others to solve a problem.

Looking at your Characteristics gives you a chance to discover "overused" strengths that could be holding you back. Fear is the number one reason we overuse a characteristic. We fear that unless we depend on that characteristic, we will be bad, unloved, lazy, judged, rejected, disrespected, and so on.

Remember Eric, the brother with two siblings? He was by nature a generous fellow. However, he overused his characteristic of generosity because he believed that not being generous all the time equaled being selfish. And it doesn't! He came to an enlightened understanding that he was generous, and yet he could also place limits on his brothers' demands without being selfish.

Exploration: Discover Your Limiting Beliefs and Vows

Look back at your list of Characteristics and write down one you think of as a strength. Remember, you aren't going to let go of this strength, you are only going to get curious about it.

What value do you assign to this Characteristic?

What are you afraid will happen if you act outside of the definition of your Characteristic?

Eric was afraid of being selfish or bad. His distorted thinking or false equivalency was: Not *always* being generous = being selfish. His enlightened thinking or understanding was: I can place limits on what favors I grant and still be a generous person.

Give it a try:

My positive character-istics	What it looks like overused	My fear	The false equivalency	A better set of choices
Persistence	Never letting go	People will think I'm a quitter	Letting go = quitting	I can choose when it makes sense to move on or try a new approach
Being generous	Not standing up for my own needs	If I stand up for myself people will think I'm being selfish	Asking for what is mine = being selfish	I can choose when to share

My positive character-istics	What it looks like overused	My fear	The false equivalency	A better set of choices

Discovering Your Limiting Beliefs
and Vows Using Turning Points

When we experience a loss in life (get divorced, sell a business, lose a friend) or a success (get accepted to graduate school, get married, buy your first house), we often develop a belief based on this experience. We make vows based on these beliefs. We can recognize a vow when we find ourselves saying, "Ever since _____ happened, I will never/always_____." Knowing what our vows are lets us choose if the belief still serves us or not.

My client, Martin, had been a "wild child," frequently serving as ringleader to his friends for all sorts of crazy activities. After college, he and a sailboat crew were caught in a storm. For him that was a turning point. As he said, "It's when I realized that I was a leader. I took control and got us all to safety." After that turning point, he became an extremely successful entrepreneur and business leader. Years later, after he had sold his company, he came upon another turning point. He was part of a problem-solving group. Most of the group was much younger, and as he recalled, "I had always believed I had to be in control to be a leader or to be of value to a group. What I realized is that I can be valuable through encouraging, mentoring, and offering a point of view. At this stage, I don't need to be in control."

Turning points don't have to be huge. When I was in college, I had the good fortune of spending two months in France and Italy with three of my cousins. It was so long ago that the guidebook entitled *Europe on 5 Dollars a Day* was still in print—and it was doable! One night in a Paris café, we met a group of French young people. One of the young men, Jean Pierre, called me after that night and took me out. It was a romantic fairy tale. He was tall, handsome, and a bit older than I. One day during a lunch beside the Seine, he asked me to go to a ball with him. "Thrilled" understates my reaction. But I had no ball gown, and buying one in Paris was not in my budget. In spite of my tears, no fairy godmother with a magic wand appeared when I got back to my hotel room. My turning point: From that day hence, I traveled with more clothes than anyone could ever need! At some point I realized this need to overpack did not serve me, and I found ways to reframe what was important to carry!

Exploration: Using Your Turning Points

Refer to the turning points in your life to complete the chart below, which will help you to finish this sentence: *Ever since that time I believed* _____.

Sometimes it helps to write out the experience first, and then write how you were before that and your new belief: See my example below.

Turning point	How you were or what you believed	Experience	New belief	Does it still serve me?
Point 1	Seeing self as a "crazy kid"	Taking control of the boat in the storm	Leaders always take control and keep everyone "safe"	No
Point 2	Being a leader who is in control	Sharing leadership with others	There are many ways to contribute my strengths as a leader	Yes

Continued on next page

Turning point	How you were or what you believed	Experience	New belief	Does it still serve me?
Point 3	I was a dawdler	My father left me cause I wasn't ready	I must ALWAYS be on time	No
Point 4				

Now it's your turn.

Turning point	How you were or what you believed	Experience	New belief	Does it still serve me?
Point 1				
Point 2				
Point 3				
Point 4				

Your vows and beliefs have existed until now in your life for good reason. But now you, your life, and the world have changed. By doing these exercises, you have given yourself the gift of awareness, and awareness gives you choices. Once I realized that I have a tendency to overwork, I became aware of the voice that tells me I have to keep pushing myself. Now, from the vantage point of my most enlightened self (I call her Big Elizabeth), I get to make the decision about whether I want to lay off or keep pushing. I've reclaimed my ability to choose.

We will always have feelings that make us uncomfortable. When you find yourself in conflict or in an uncomfortable situation, just ask yourself: *Is this hooking into vows and beliefs that I made long ago to keep me safe? Might those beliefs and vows be distorting my decision-making powers now? Are these beliefs and vows inhibiting my ability to act in ways that serve me well?*

Warning: Questioning these beliefs and vows can kick up your Triple J. These vows and beliefs may have become almost as powerful as religion. If the Triple J begins to talk loudly against you when you challenge these long-held vows, your best defense is awareness. Don't try to make the voice go away, just be aware that it is there. Often the Triple J is the loudest when we are moving toward freedom and transcendence. (Go back to Chapter 1 for the Rx Antibiotic for the Triple J.)

If the Triple J is really loud, or if you feel like you could use a few more explorations to root out those pieces that could be keeping you from the life you envision, here are two explorations that will help you see even more clearly. Because false equivalencies and vicious cycles can be some of the most obstinate obstacles to living large, the explorations are based on them. Have fun exploring!

Exploration: Finding Your False Equivalencies

Here are some common beginnings of false equivalencies. See what comes up when you finish the sentences. Just seeing the false equivalency in print can send it packing:

- If I have money, then ...

- If I were better looking, then ...

- If I set a boundary with my friends/coworker/sibling/ spouse, then ...

- If I worked less, then ...

- If I state what I want ...

Remember, it's okay to want to have and do things. Just be clear with yourself about the beliefs underlying those aspirations. And yes, it's even okay to aspire to have just a little. But make sure you're not settling for less than you want or deserve through a false equivalency that says wanting makes you a bad person ...

Ex: If I (add an action)	Then (state the negative conclusion or consequence)	T/F
1. If I set limits	then I'm being a dictator	
2. If I choose to leave	then I'm a quitter	
3. If I question someone's intentions	then I'm suspicious/mistrusting	
4. If I ask for help	then I'm lazy/incompetent	
5. If I disagree with someone	then they may not like me	

Ex: If I (add an action)	Then (state the negative conclusion or consequence)	T/F
1. If I	then	
2. If I	then	
3. If I	then	
4. If I	then	
5. If I	then	

Recently, one of my clients, a talented and experienced PR professional, started her own PR firm with a trusted partner. Prior to that, she'd worked in New York for big-name publishers, celebrities, *New York Times* best-selling authors, and had even done a stint with Oprah! Her resume was impressive. Now she has a company that is doing very well. Sales are growing, and they are making money and adding employees. Yet in spite of their success, she doesn't *feel successful*. After doing this exercise, she realized she equates success with having celebrity clients. With that insight, she was able to see that she already has the success she really wants—a trusted partner, a profitable business, a flexible schedule, and freedom from corporate politics. Whether we realize it or not, false equivalencies are lies we believe that limit our lives. Routing them out is powerful work and can lead to tremendous freedom.

Exploration: Breaking Your Cycles

By filling in the chart below, you can quickly uncover some of those vicious self-sabotaging cycles that may have taken up residence and are blocking your ability to live as large as you want to.

1. Are there things that seem to be happening again and again in your life? Feelings you have had? Things you say a lot? ("I work all the time," "He never listens to me," "I feel like I can never keep up.") Write them down.

2. What is the belief you have about this? Write this in the first gray box on p.99.

3. What action(s) do you take based on that belief? Put that in the second box(es).

4. What are the results of that action? Put that in the third box. The action may trigger responses from others or an emotional response from you. Sometimes writing a "because" statement about it can help. Other times writing an "and that means" statement can help. ("I work all the time, because it is the only way to make enough money to pay the bills." "If I don't do it, it won't get done." "He never listens to me, and that means he doesn't love me.")

5. Continue on around the circle (Vicious Cycle), mapping out a response and what that action or feeling elicits. It will eventually bring you back around to the unproductive behavior or situation you want to stop!

6. Pause a moment. Can you see that your belief is perpetuating the cycle?

7. Once you have mapped out the cycle, you can choose to change your response. Once you do, then what follows will change—maybe not overnight, but it will change. You and only you have the power to turn a Vicious Cycle into a virtuous one.

8. Write down the one change you will make to change the cycle.

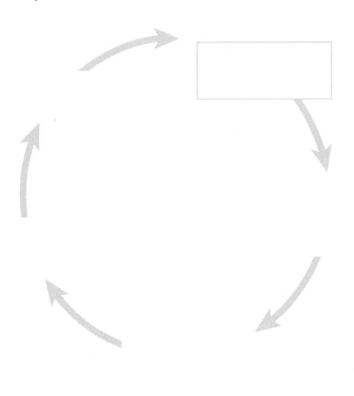

Advanced Exploration (Optional): What Keeps the Vicious Cycle in Place

Once you have identified the belief statement, you can use the following chart to jettison the belief.

1. Write the belief down.

2. Ask: Is it true? Could it be that this is a false and Limiting Belief?

3. Write a new belief statement: "I can find ways to work less and still make the money I want." "He loves me, but he may need me to say things differently in order to really hear me." Be willing to be a little bit uncomfortable here as you marshal the courage to change your beliefs.

4. Practice doing this over and over in the following chart with anything in your life that feels a little stuck. This is a cycle. It has momentum and stability of its own accord.

Old belief	New belief

CHAPTER 10

The Label Trap

W hen you picked up this book, you made a kind of declaration: "I want to live as full and rich a life as I possibly can!" "I want to create possibilities I might not have imagined before." "I want to use my talents, experience, and resources in an intentional way." "I want to Live Large in this next stage of my life." Your work in Section I made explicit the foundational pieces of who you are, why you are here (purpose), and what guides your life (values). The work you just did on Limiting Beliefs was the most challenging because it invited you to call into question assumptions about yourself and your place in the world. Now that we have learned to jettison those limits, we can focus on what works, where you are strong, what you know how to do, and your unique talents that can be leveraged to help you reach great heights at the end of the Live Large process.

We start by identifying the difference between your Know-Whats and your Know-Hows. This is an amazing exploration that can take you from CEO to best-selling how-to author; stay-at-home mom to successful "momtrepreneur"; business executive to business coach; nonprofit middle manager to NGO fund-raiser.

The first thing you need to know about moving from Know-What to Know-How is that your job title does not define you. Ever since we were little, people have asked us, "What do you want to be when you grow up?" The question gets repeated again and again throughout high school, college, and beyond. We get accustomed to thinking about work in terms of our job titles—*I want to be a software developer, business owner, banker, photographer, pilot, nurse*—and what industries we work in—*I am in financial services, healthcare, manufacturing, retail, wholesale, technology, etc.* There's nothing wrong with identifying with our profession or industry. It gives us a way of naming ourselves and contributes to our sense of identity, security, and pride. We're a *this*, not a *that*. It can also be a source of embarrassment (*I'm only a _____*).

Either way, the label can become a trap. We begin to believe if we are a _____, then we will always be a _____. And when we start thinking about a change, our options feel limited.

One of my most recent clients, a sweet young redhead named Cady, came to me when she was tired of her career running a high-end men's retail store in Seattle. "Running a store like this is the only thing I know how to do," she told me despairingly. Cady's real challenge was not knowing her "What" from her "How."

Your Know-Whats are the specifics of what you are doing in a particular context. For example, are you skilled at giving dinner parties? Your Know-What could be serving a chicken dinner for eight. Other Know-Whats: grilling the chicken, roasting potatoes, tossing a salad, making corn on the cob, and serving peaches and ice cream for dessert. Know-Whats are tangible and easy to identify. They also have the ability to either free you or trap you. It's easy to fall into the Know-What trap. From the time we first start school we are continuously being tested on what we know: *What is 2+2? When was the Magna Carta signed? Recite the Gettysburg Address.* Then, as adults: *Do you know the product line, the current HR policy, the biggest challenges and opportunities facing your industry?* All of this is about what you know. There is so much emphasis placed upon it that we may come to believe that *what* we know is *all* we know. If we believe that, we will feel trapped in the same industry we've always been in, because it's what we know.

Cady, who was getting really tired of being in retail, came to realize that underneath the Know-Whats of her daily activities, she had a repertoire of skills—her "Know-Hows"—she had previously dismissed under the heading of *managing a men's clothing store.* With these skills she could do much more than manage a store. Here is a list of Cady's skills:

* Interview and hire staff

* Manage and motivate people

* Schedule resources to accomplish a task

* Establish priorities

* Facilitate communication between a corporate headquarters and an external location

* Develop and write up procedures

* Create programs to engage potential customers

* Analyze market segments

* Understand what customers are looking for

- Create structure

- Define a sales process

- Sell products and ideas

- Source products

- Develop and manage budgets

- Network within an industry

What Cady didn't realize was that hidden in the Know-Whats of her daily activities were a bunch of Know-Hows. And those Know-Hows would eventually lead her into the career of her dreams. The same may be true for you. Your definition of what you think you can do is probably a lot narrower than what you can actually do. Whether you realize it or not, over the years you have accumulated a lot of knowledge and skills—your Know-Hows— and becoming aware of them can be both eye-opening and inspiring: You get to see yourself in a whole new way. In fact, you might realize you could run a small country with everything you know how to do!

You may be able to grill a chicken—that's your Know-What. But the processes that go into making that chicken dinner are your Know-Hows, and these open up possibilities and let you escape from the industry, job, or role you no longer want. If you can make a chicken dinner for eight, you also know how to:

- Assess a situation and generate options (how many people, what's fresh in the market, food sensitivities, etc.)

- Assemble components required to create a final product (shop)

- Execute a set of written instructions (follow the recipe)

- Coordinate various timetables to achieve a result (figure out that if the chicken takes twenty-five minutes to grill and the corn takes three, then the salad should be dressed after the corn is in the pot and just before you eat, etc.)

- Assure the availability and appropriateness of tools and equipment to do the job (the grill is hot and has gas/charcoal, there is a big pot to hold the corn, a sharp knife to peel the peaches, etc.)

- Set expectations for delivery (tell people dinner will be ready at 7:30)

Know-Hows are exponentially important because they expand the possibilities of what you can offer in the world. Now it's your turn to figure out the Know-Whats and Know-Hows of your life!

Exploration: Your Know-Whats and Your Know-Hows

In this exploration, you will dig deeper into your own Know-Whats and Know-Hows. As you move through the exercise, remember that the *whats* are often tangible and industry specific—think specific job titles—while the *hows* are more process oriented. For example, journalism might be the Know-What, but writing, editing, gathering facts, and assembling them is the Know-How. Customer Service in an air-conditioning business is a Know-What. Knowing what questions to ask for an initial assessment, creating an action plan, and dealing with an irate customer is the process—the Know-How. If you are a senior executive in a bank, your Know-What may be finance or commercial lending, but your Know-Hows can include developing client relationships, creating a company culture, and mentoring midlevel managers. You get the picture.

Fill out all the Know-Whats below. Start by looking at your earliest positions, and be sure to include volunteer activities. Examples could include: seller of Girl Scout cookies, gymnast, Estée Lauder perfume girl, administrative assistant for an arts organization, social media marketer for an environmental protection organization, etc.

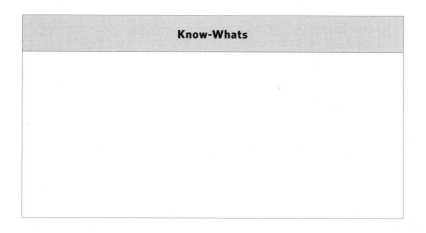

Independent of a specific job or industry, your Know-Hows may be hard to find at first. Use your list of Know-Whats to guide you toward them, keeping the chicken dinner example from earlier in mind. What are all of the skills you used in each position you've held?

My daughter Sarah had just about had it with her job with a

large beverage distribution company, where she managed tens of thousands of products going to dozens of distributors. In spite of the accolades she received, she said, "I have to get out of there. It's making me crazy!"

As she looked at her Know-Whats and Know-Hows, she realized she knew not just about the beverage industry, but also about distribution and logistics. She excelled at putting people and resources together to get a job done. She also knew how to see the big picture and break it down into its component pieces. As we talked, I reminded her of a story I had told many times:

"When you were in grade school, you and I used to go to the theater together. One of the first times we went, I asked what you thought. Figuring a nine-year-old would say, 'Great,' I was amazed when you replied, 'Overall the show was good, I'm so glad we came.' Then you proceeded to make specific suggestions about the staging, the costumes, the acting, and the music. I was astonished."

Sarah's ability to see how the individual pieces can come together to create a larger whole is a Know-How she's had for a long time. Knowing this gave her lots of choices, and she soon found her next job handling national accounts for a logistics company.

Now it's your turn. When identifying your Know-Hows, think as creatively as you can from the bottom up. Where are processes hiding that can be extracted? What skills can you use, regardless of setting? If you were a middle child, you may have developed skills in harmonizing conflicting interests. Have you seen that emerging in your work? Claim it. If you feel stuck, just close your eyes and ask your guide to give you a word of advice. Everything wants you to grow, evolve, and move into a place that feels satisfying.

Know-Hows

Whenever you feel limited about taking the next step, this list is a resource for you. If you are about to offer your services to a new or existing client or are about to switch jobs, this list of your Know-Hows is vital in helping others to see your unique value. Even if you want your life to look very different, these are areas of expertise you can carry with you from industry to industry. They can open doors for you in surprising ways when you move them forward into the world.

But here's something to watch out for: You may have a list of Know-Hows, but only some of them might feel exciting and fun to you. Have you ever noticed that you can be working on something and the next time you look up, an hour has passed? Or even after a full day of work, you have that "tired but happy" feeling? I get that when I'm facilitating a problem-solving session with a team, designing a strategic planning retreat, or working one-on-one with a client. I may be physically tired, especially if I've been on my feet all day, but I feel good, satisfied, and energized.

Doing things that energize us will yield a high "Yippee Index®." This is a term I made up to illustrate how jazzed we can get about a situation. On a scale of one to five, going skiing or working with a client are both fives on my Yippee Index, while dealing with a full inbox or a technology glitch are ones (or minus ones!).

A few years ago, I visited a resort island in Fiji with fourteen guest cabins, or *bures*. The grounds were pristine, and the cabins—elegant in their simplicity—came equipped with only the bare necessities: a clean and comfortable bed, a hammock, a constant breeze, a view of the water, and a place for washing the sand off my feet. Staff came from neighboring islands and spent twelve days on and four days off the island, so the same smiling faces greeted me for the entirety of my stay.

It was interesting to see how many jobs the staff had. The person who greeted me at breakfast also tidied up the room or did laundry. The young man who swept up the sea grape leaves around my *bure* sang lead in the group that played at night and entertained at lunch. On Saturday night, he and two other young men with guitars and a ukulele sang a mix of Fijian songs and American tunes as varied as "Bring It On Home" to "I Can't Stop Loving You," an occasional John Denver song, and "Swing Low, Sweet Chariot." Some of us danced the Fijian shuffle, a side-by-side dance apparently introduced by the missionaries to discourage face-to-face engagement (but no doubt leading to a more intimate exchange).

After singing and dancing until almost midnight, I was surprised first thing the next morning to see the three guitar-playing singers out raking leaves, keeping my *bure* and my part of the beach pristine. Masi, the lead singer with a big voice and beautiful harmonies, burst into a smile when I asked him how he was able to sing so late at night and be up early enough to rake the leaves. He patted his chest, "The music is in my heart. I love it." I thought about that. And then I had another question. I understood how he had the energy to stay up late and sing, but what gave him the energy to get up the following morning? Masi shook his head as if he were explaining the obvious to a child. "Doing what you love gives you the energy to do everything else."

What energizes you is absolutely any activity you do that makes you feel stronger, happier, and more connected. When Cady, the one who managed a men's retail store, reflected upon her list of Know-Hows, she saw that much of what energized her actually happened outside of work, like attending art shows, leading bike tours around Seattle, and organizing groups of friends for themed parties. If you can identify and move toward what energizes you, you will undoubtedly have adequate energy left over for the rest of your Know-Hows that may be necessary to live large.

Exploration: Energize Your Life

In this exploration you will divide your list of Know-Hows into two categories according to what energizes you—what you most look forward to doing—and what depletes you—what leaves you tired and grumpy. Do you love creating a plan, organizing details, developing a new process, mentoring a new employee or younger friend, writing code, solving a mechanical problem, socializing, or managing a project to completion? Put these in the "energizing activities" box. The goal here is to help you maximize those activities in your life and minimize what depletes you. When what you do feeds you, absolutely anything is possible.

Energizing activities	Depleting activities

CHAPTER 11

Innately Gifted, Wildly Talented YOU

Unlike the Know-Whats and the Know-Hows, talents and gifts are not skills we have developed. Rather, they are abilities that come naturally to us, things we have been doing in one way or another all our lives. For instance, I've always perceived patterns and connections. It was only in my forties that I began to realize this was a unique talent. I'd assumed because I did it, everyone did. Similarly, my husband has had gustatory memory for much of his life: He can eat a meal or dish and recall it decades later or read a recipe and know what it will taste like. Because it comes naturally to him, he may not realize that not everyone has this gift. Another example: People who are outgoing struggle to understand those who are shy.

Sometimes we are profoundly irreverent about our talents and gifts, but more often than not we don't even know they are there. My friend Martha has a gift for connection and hospitality. In any room, either business or social, she knows who should talk to whom and how it will be good for both of them. Does she plot it out? No. She just does it. When I tell her she has a real gift, she dismisses me with, "It's nothing." Like most of us, she figures if something comes so easily, then it must not be special. Many of us live with the mistaken belief: *If it's not hard, it's not valuable.*

Marcus Buckingham, noted speaker and author of many books, says it's best to focus on the things that make us feel stronger rather than weaker. This often feels counterintuitive in our culture. Most of my life and probably yours, parents, teachers, bosses, and indeed you yourself have most likely focused on improving your "weaknesses." *If I could just improve x, y, or z . . .* I don't know what part of our culture motivated us to look at improving our weaknesses instead of working on what makes us feel strong. In my own family, it had to do with striving for perfection (talk about something that will deplete you!).

Our gifts can energize us. If we look for them, they show themselves in all parts of our lives. My daughter Sarah is an incredible writer. When my parents celebrated their fiftieth wedding anniversary, our family made a scrapbook for them, and each child and grandchild wrote a page of his or her thoughts and memories. Sarah was fourteen, the next-to-youngest contributor. Her piece was funny, clever, tender, and one of the best in the book. It took her less than an hour to write, while her college-aged, equally smart brother hemmed and hawed for a couple of days.

"Sarah," I told her, "the piece you wrote for Granny and Pop was wonderful. You have a real talent for writing."

She replied with a shrug, "It's no big deal. Writing is easy. When you finish one sentence, the next one just pops into place." It reminded me of what my friend and successful songwriter Marshall Chapman once told me about one of her songs: "It just came to me in fifteen minutes." Of course, she still has to work at her writing like everyone else. Someone may be a musical prodigy with perfect pitch, but without the skill and discipline of formal study, she will fall short of what she might have done. But Marshall is talented. And so is Sarah.

Not only do we not recognize our gifts, we often dismiss them, as Sarah did. We hear the message early on: *No pain, no gain.* So when something is easy for us, we believe it must not be valuable or special.

Earlier in my career, when I was working in organization development in Caracas, I was invited to join a small group of brilliant psychoanalysts, writers, and professors to meet and discuss the work of a visiting author and practitioner. I felt timid speaking, but I did it anyway. The next week, I met with the analyst who had invited me to the event. "You offered such a fresh, intelligent perspective whenever you contributed," she told me. "What I noticed, though, was that you began your comments with, 'I'm probably wrong, but . . .'"

I believed *either* everyone else saw the point I was making *or* I was wrong. It has taken me years to recognize and then embrace that I have gifts and talents—and so do you!

Exploration: Innately Gifted, Wildly Talented YOU

Knowing that you have been "gifted" since birth with unique strengths gives you power and leads to a high Yippee Index and a rich life. We want to shine a light of awareness on your talents and gifts, just as we did your Limiting Beliefs, in order to give you more choices. These innate talents can be potent resources. Once you find a way to leverage them, work takes on a fluid feel. You have probably observed someone who seems very relaxed when he or she is working, despite being in a demanding situation. The strain is gone. He's utilizing his innate genius. People like to be around a person like that. We want to hire/contract/partner with that person. Exploring your talents and gifts brings you one step closer toward being this type of successful individual.

Before you begin, ask your friends to identify areas in which you excel. Listen and take notes. Take it all in. Many of us are so indoctrinated to diminish our talents that it can be hard for us to articulate them. But your friends have been watching, and they can be your best resources for this exploration.

My son Rob has been organizing people for various endeavors since he was a kid, when he brought the other kids on the block together to make a movie. Since then, he has created a team-based challenge course in grad school, organized a seventeen-day white-water paddle trip for other enthusiasts, built momentum for a greenway project, and is now growing an office in South Carolina for a Canadian firm. Getting people together and motivated to make something happen is a talent he has. What is a role you've been playing "all of your life," since you were a kid?

Beware of your Triple J during this exploration! As you begin to discern your talents and gifts, the diminishing and invalidating voice of your Triple J will tell you, "That's not special; anybody can do that." This exercise expands horizons and bursts through limitations, and the Triple J hates that. You know if the Triple J is trying to burn a hole through your list, you are doing excellent work. Either ignore that voice, write down what it's saying, or if it is just too loud, talk (yell) back at it!

Look back at those times you've lost track of time or activities that come easily that you enjoy. Cady, the men's retail sales manager, realized that she was gifted at getting people excited about what she had to offer. This had served her well in sales, and it had made her a sort of social pied piper: People wanted to be where Cady was. Now, reference your list of Know-Hows and use the chart below to identify your talents:

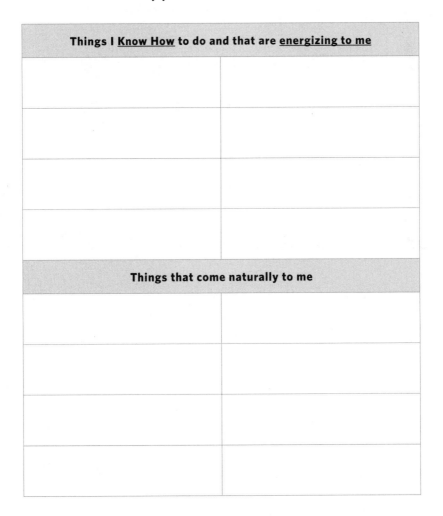

Things I **Know How** to do and that are **energizing to me**	
Things that come naturally to me	

Things people say I'm good at	

Reflection: What do I notice? What are the themes?	

My talents!!!!	

Cady was an artist at heart. Keeping in mind her unique gifts for connecting and socializing, she approached a successful Seattle sculptor and asked if he was interested in expanding his market and the impact of his art. She used her promoting and selling skills to paint a vision for him of what they could create together. Now she uses her organizational skills every day, operating a space for artists complete with studios and galleries. She used her Know-How of creating events, networking, promoting, and selling to create a real community hotspot, a place to go for food, wine, and some of the best art in the city. By identifying what she knew how to do, where her talents were, and what energized her, Cady was able to create a whole new career.

• • •

Once you reflect on which of your Know-Hows energize you most, your gifts and talents emerge. And once you know them, you are able to enrich the criteria for the work and life that will make you feel enormous in terms of impact and inspiration. Does this mean you have to be talented at everything you do at work, or that everything has to be energizing? No. Think about Masi: He probably loved to sing more than he loved to sweep, but one gave him energy for the other.

Try to keep your list of talents and gifts at the forefront of your mind, especially as you move through this process. You are incredibly gifted and unique. You have essential, innate gifts that are effortless. And while certainly we like to add skills and hard work to those innate talents, the gifts aren't going anywhere, and you can rely on them as you move into the final section of the book and look at some of the most exciting parts of the Live Large process:

what roles you want to play, who you really want to be, what you've always wanted to have, what you'd like to accomplish, and the huge impact you want to make in the world.

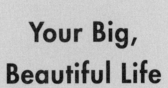
Your Big,
Beautiful Life

"Faced with the choice between changing
one's mind and proving that there is no need to do so,
almost everyone gets busy on the proof."
—John Kenneth Galbraith

"In this life we cannot do great things.
We can only do small things with great love."
—Mother Teresa

CHAPTER 12

The Bull's-eye

Over the years, people who have participated in my Live Large planning sessions have said things like:

> The other day, I was cleaning out my desk when I came across the exercise you had us do in the workshop: the Bull's-eye. Well, I'm embarrassed to say that after the workshop, even though I was excited, some things came up and I never looked at the paper again. But here's the thing you'll never believe. When I looked at the Bull's-eye, I was amazed to see how many of the things I had written down had happened. I could hardly believe my eyes!

One of the most important steps you'll take in your journey toward Living Large, the Bull's-eye is about expansive thinking: not just about your career, but about everything your life holds. In creating your Bull's-eye, you will increase the odds of getting what you want by actually writing it down. The exercise creates a holistic picture of all that you are aiming for: the new house you will live in, the book you will write, the mountain you will climb, the spouse you will love, and so on. It's a creative vision for all the ways you want to show up in the world and leave an impact. Depending on your age, you may even think of it as your legacy.

The Bull's-eye is a way of bringing together who we are in our many roles and what we want to have, accomplish, be, and impact in those roles. The Bull's-eye is not just a single red dot in the middle of the board—it's the whole board, inclusive of every role you play now, and may play in the future. The roles we play often feel separate from one another. We are parents, spouses, businesspeople, community leaders, volunteers, athletes, artists, writers, and so on, and we long for a way to bring these roles together. The Bull's-eye helps us find ways to allow our roles to act in synergy with one another.

I recently used the Bull's-eye with a husband and wife team who were feeling exhausted by their business. Dean and his wife Shana had started an engineering company when they were just out of college. Twenty years later, they had two boys in grade school and a company with twenty-five employees. Both sets of parents lived near their small Midwestern town, and they cherished their time as a family. When they called me, they were feeling overwhelmed and thought it might be time to sell their business. The Bull's-eye helped them gain clarity about what they wanted next.

We started the exercise by outlining the roles that were important to each of them. In his role as a business leader, Dean wanted to bring other businesspeople together to work on community and regional environmental initiatives. In his role as a family member, he wanted to spend time with his family and be able to take them on trips. In his role as a community influencer, he wanted to continue volunteering with youth and preserving the wildlife around his house. In her roles as an artist, teacher, and family member, Shana wanted time to create and sell art, teach a weekly Sunday school class, and take trips with her children and her parents.

In order for Dean to fulfill his desired role as a community leader, he needed the platform a successful business provided him, so we didn't want to dismantle their business too soon. However, he also wanted some relief from the time commitment it required of him. Shana, on the other hand, wanted out of the daily work of the business altogether. By working through the Bull's-eye, they determined a joint need to develop a stronger team who could handle some of their new projects so they could pursue other roles that were important to them.

Dean went on to hire an operations manager and let go of a few employees he'd had to "babysit." With this new structure, the business started doing extremely well. Shana is out of the business, but because she's an excellent big-picture thinker, she still sits on the board. Now, she's had the time to do something she'd longed to do since college: study the visual arts. She's painted portraits of her boys, and several of her friends have asked her to paint their children as well. Meanwhile, Dean isn't overwhelmed at work anymore and has since joined a regional chamber of commerce and the regional Boy Scout council. The pair took their boys to California with Dean's parents last year and are planning a trip to New York with her parents next year. They've already taken two "couples weekends" this year, which has made their relationship thrive. Their success story demonstrates how tweaking aspects of one role can have a dramatic impact on all others.

Sometimes one of our roles is mutually exclusive of another, and we must choose which to prioritize. Sally, a manager for a high-end book distribution company, came to me because she loved poker. She loved the psychology of the game, and she had fun tracking and analyzing her results. By the time I met with her, she'd gained a hot reputation in the amateur club scene, and club owners were beginning to stake her in order to bring in high-quality players. She was thinking about going pro.

When Sally and I worked through the Bull's-eye, she expressed a willingness to change parts of her lifestyle in order to become a professional poker player—for instance, as a night owl, she was unfazed by the game's late-night hours. However, as we dug deeper, she realized that the inevitable move to Las Vegas would get in the way of every other role she wanted to play in her life, including her role as a dedicated spouse, an engaged member of her extended family, and her future role as a mom. The other role she enjoyed was that of an enthusiastic athlete. She played on the city volleyball and softball teams and loved being part of her community. Participation in these sports would be tougher if she were playing poker every night. In the end Sally decided that playing poker would remain an avocation—something she enjoyed and could continue to improve. Going through the Bull's-eye exercise gave her what she needed to make the right choice for her . . . one she could feel good about.

Gaining clarity about the roles that are important to us helps us define our lives in a holistic and realistic way. Instead of getting stuck thinking we have to throw out our business, or make poker the end-all be-all, we can place our lives in a larger frame—and the Bull's-eye helps us do just that.

Exploration: The Bull's-eye

On the following pages you'll find two Bull's-eye charts: one that has been filled out as a sample and another one that's blank and ready to hold all of your ideas about what you want in your life in the upcoming years. Let's get started.

On the midline, list four to six roles you would like to play in the next three to five years. Considering the roles you *want* to play, rather than the ones you have been playing, allows you to discern where you are heading and whether there are roles you may want to phase out or stop giving so much attention to. These roles might be very concrete and specific, or they can be symbolic and metaphorical, but they are the ones that are important to you—the ones you want to focus on. These might include: business owner, community volunteer, musician, artist, caregiver, athlete, parent, coach, family member, intellectual, spiritual being, change agent, benefactor, dreamer of dreams, poet, convener, defender of the disadvantaged, advocate, inventor, inspirer, writer (I had to add that to my circle!). Consolidate roles where possible to keep the list small: Parent, spouse, and caregiver can be consolidated into *family member*. Volunteer, community leader, and advocate may combine into *community player*. Using the example as a reference, write one role in each "ring" of your Bull's-eye. It doesn't matter which role goes in which ring.

My Future 3–5 Years

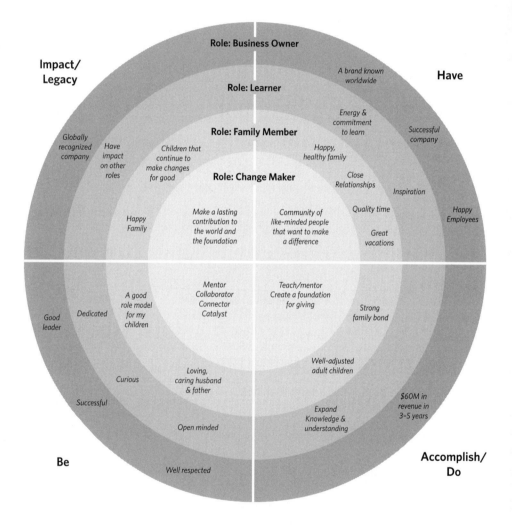

My Future 3-5 Years

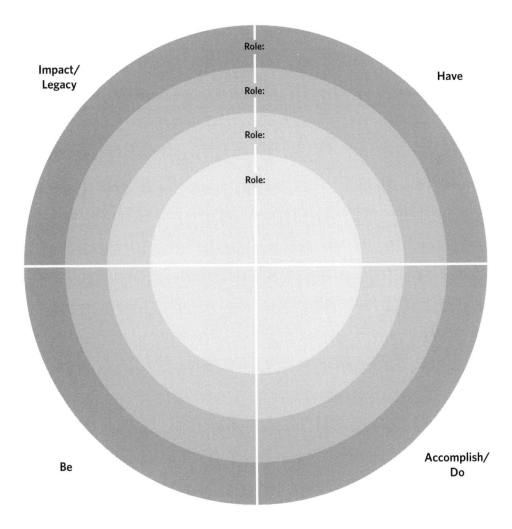

Chart adopted by permission from the
Institute of Cultural Affairs

The Four Quadrants of Your Bull's-eye

Now that you have figured out what roles you want to be playing three to five years from now, ask yourself what you want to have, accomplish, be, and impact within each role. Some people put a few words in each section, while others have to write very small to fit in everything they want to say. Whichever you choose is right for you. The *"haves"* may be tangible: a house, your own business, or a child. Or they may be something less tangible: good health, close friends, a sense of possibility, and optimism. For example, if "family member" is one of your roles, you might list a child, or a beach house your grandkids can come to, in your "Have" section. "Haves" can also be specific to your business or work life. You may list a business coach or an Internet marketing team so you can spend more time with family and less time at the office. Here are some other examples of "haves" for your Bull's-eye:

- My first child

- A house of my own

- A family reunion

- A strategy for high-impact investing

- A salary of more than $_____

- A new facility for my company

- Recognition for my research

Now move down one quadrant in your Bull's-eye and ask yourself: What do you want to *accomplish* within that role? What are your goals and aspirations? Don't be afraid to be ambitious. Jot down the ideas that have been with you for a long time. It's okay to think big, but it's also okay to stay small. Here are a few examples of what you might accomplish in a given role:

- Write a book

- Learn a foreign language

- Climb a mountain

- Spend Sundays with my grandkids

- Interview at least six people I admire in my field

- Fund or found an organization

- Compete in a marathon

- Perform a one-woman show

- Serve on the board of a publicly traded company

- Hold a patent

- Send my children to college

- Go to the gym three times a week

Only you know what you want to accomplish. And remember, this is about what *you* want, not what a parent, teacher, spouse, or sibling has said you should accomplish.

Moving over to the next quadrant, ask yourself: What do you want to *be* in each role? We often think that if we have or do the right things, then we'll be loved, admired, respected, and so on. However, when we seek to "have" or "do" *in order to* be loved, feel safe, or gain respect, we may find ourselves with a house full of stuff and a long list of accomplishments, yet still lacking the sense of peace that we believed would come. Thus, this section is about answering the question: How will this role—and who I will be in this role—make me feel good, complete, satisfied, enough? It also describes you as your most authentic self—the person fulfilling your purpose and living your values.

Here are some examples of "*be's*" you might include in your Bull's-eye:

- Sought after for my creativity
- Loved and respected
- A recognized authority in my industry
- A catalyst for change
- Content with what I have
- A loving spouse
- A good example for my children

Now, let's move to the fourth quadrant. Ask yourself: How can you make an *impact* in each of the roles you play? How will what you do make a difference after you are no longer around? We are not necessarily talking about after death—we are talking about leaving a legacy once it's time to move on. We are talking about ways you can not only affect the world, but change it as well. Impacts can be small or big. What's key is that they matter to you.

Have you ever walked through the snow or across a damp beach and seen your footprints linger behind you? Your step made an impact: It changed what was there before. If you step into wet cement, your impact will be preserved for a longer time. If you mentor a young person, your impact will last far beyond your engagement. However large or small, each of our actions leaves an impact, even if we are not able to see its full extent. Here are some examples of ways you might leave an impact:

- A safer community
- A volunteer program
- A close-knit family
- A business that can operate without me
- A team that is skilled and confident
- A major gift to my university

The Distillation

Now it's time to look at that center mark in your Bull's-eye. You may want to fiddle with this on a separate document or piece of paper first. Check out everything you have written in your four quadrants for each of the roles you want to play. If you had to distill it all down to three or four phrases that capture what you want in the next three to five years of your life, what would you say? Don't struggle with this: Just see what begins to emerge. Imagine you are telling this to your best friend or spouse: What would you say? If it doesn't just pop out immediately, don't worry. The ideas are in your subconscious somewhere and will begin to emerge soon enough. Here are some examples I've seen:

- Loving and connected family
- Active, fit, and full of energy
- Making a difference in my community

- Sharing my resources to make a difference
- Shaping the future of my profession, my family, my community, my _____
- Giving my creativity free reign
- Engaged with a vibrant professional community
- Financial responsibility and predictability
- A good steward for my family
- Growing a company I'm proud of
- Preparing the next generation
- Welcoming joy
- Deep intention in my choices
- Leader and follower
- Breaking down barriers
- Fulfilling my potential
- Challenging what is
- Creating opportunities

Overall, when you look at each role and what you want to have/accomplish/be/impact, what are you really aiming for? In some ways the sentences in the middle of your Bull's-eye read like a postcard from the future. Armed with these key sentences, you're akin to a traveler keeping a picture of his or her next destination.

• • •

Put your Bull's-eye somewhere special so you can continue to remind yourself what you are aiming for. In our next chapters, we will get concrete about how you are going to get there.

My distillation

CHAPTER 13

Where Do You Want to Play?

"If you don't know where you're going," the famous saying goes, "any road will lead you there." Developing criteria for what you want is key to taking the next step toward a bigger, more rewarding life—one that brings together and makes use of all your skills, talents, and resources. I learned the importance of criteria in graduate school. In an afternoon workshop we had to develop a "product" using Tinker Toys and hold a demonstration to promote it. Competition was keen (think *Project Runway*); secrecy and industrial espionage ran amuck. I was on a great team of high-energy, creative people. We were bursting with ideas as we raced against the clock to plan and build the perfect product. As the last grains of sand drained through the hourglass, we stood up and shouted *Yes!* This was our moment! Victory!

Years later, I can no longer remember what our product was

or how we promoted it, but I do remember my sense of certainty that our product was best and that my team had won. But we hadn't! After the winner was announced, there was an unspoken but palpable bewilderment (dare I say indignation?). *What were the judges thinking?*

Ah, that indeed was the question, what *were* the judges thinking? Sensing our team's frustration, our professor asked us if we were surprised by the decision. Some of us nodded, trying hard not to express how cheated we felt. He smiled a sly smile. "We had criteria for the product and criteria for the presentation."

"Oh, what were they?" we asked.

It turned out the product that used the most pieces and was built the tallest got the most points, and the presentation had to include singing and dancing to be eligible to win. "What's really interesting," he continued, "is that none of you asked what the criteria were for success."

His words have stayed with me ever since.

What are your criteria for the situations in which you want to work, play, be creative, be a leader? In this chapter, we'll focus on identifying the characteristics for your work situation, but this exploration is also valuable for any situation. Answering this question is tricky because the lives we say we want often aren't what we are truly looking for. We become attracted to certain companies, industries, or a particular job without ever asking if the characteristics of the situation are right. We like the *idea* of it more than we like the reality.

Matthew was an unassuming midcareer engineer with soft blue eyes and an MBA from an Ivy League school. For most of his career, he'd enjoyed working as a project manager for companies in the aerospace industry. Because he hated the interruptions from other engineers who needed help when their projects were behind schedule, he thought the solution was to be his own boss. He borrowed money from his family and bought a small tool and die business, where he would have control over the projects and avoid interruptions. It was a disaster almost from the get-go.

There were major trends in his industry he hadn't researched, and shortly after taking over, one of his largest accounts stopped doing business altogether. Things went from bad to worse. After several frustrating and expensive years, he closed the company and came to me for help. When I asked him what he most loved to do, he said, "I like to get my nose into a technical problem and stick with it until I have it solved."

When we were identifying the characteristics he wanted in his work life, he said, "I like stability of work flow so I can schedule my time accordingly. And I don't like to manage other people, I just want to work on interesting projects without interruption."

Bingo. We had simultaneously identified his criteria and reason he had failed at owning his own business. Any small business owner will tell you the keys to success are the ability to manage people and deal with changing gears frequently—two things he hated. His business failed, but that's okay because figuring out what he wanted wound up being priceless. Once you figure out the characteristics for what you want, you'll be way ahead in developing options, and options are the key to taking the next step.

When I was running a start-up division for a midsized company, I did a lot of hiring. I knew a start-up wasn't for everybody, and it was important to talk to people about what sort of environment really got their juices flowing. Some folks loved to figuratively walk into an empty space with building supplies lying around. It was exciting for them to imagine what could be built and how they would use the resources to create something fantastic. Other people found this sort of empty space or unstructured environment stressful. A surprising number of people said they'd never been asked about how they liked to work and under what conditions they worked best.

I had a brilliant friend, Alex, who had two degrees from Yale and one from Stanford. He'd been an executive VP in a well-established overseas financial firm and subsequently worked internationally for one of the premier consulting firms in the world. Because he wanted to settle down in one place, he and his family returned to the United States, where he established an independent consulting practice. When he came to me, he was depressed. Without the structure of an organization, he floundered. He had trouble structuring his day, and his engagements felt unproductive and inefficient. It was clear he needed to work for someone else, to move within the context of another company's structural flow.

There's no good or bad, right or wrong about whether you want to work alone or as part of a team, seek daily challenges or predictable work, be boss or not. What is important is understanding which situations are most rewarding and stimulating to you as an individual. When you know what you want, you can go after it with greater intention.

Exploration: Characteristics of the Work Situation You Want

This is a time to let go and brainstorm the characteristics, qualities, and aspects you want in your work environment. Go wild, reach for the sky, think quantity not quality. If it feels like fantasy, that's probably your Triple J talking . . . don't begin editing this list too soon.

Get it all down on paper first! It's easier to create more now and take away ideas later rather than to staunch the flow of creativity.

Do you prefer a quiet, uninterrupted work environment or someplace where something new is happening all the time? Do you get stressed or energized when critical decisions must be made quickly? Do you want to be running whatever show you are in or supporting a great leader? Sometimes personality profiles like DiSC or Meyers Briggs (MBTI) can include insights you have about the kind of work situation that would best fit your style.

Here are some of the characteristics I have heard from different people:

Work alone	Work as intensely as I would like	Be my own boss	More writing
Be part of a team	Really want to use my brain	Fixed compensation	Freedom to take a trip
Want to be the boss	See people face-to-face	Rewarded based on my results	Manager that can operate almost without me
No travel	Large, prestigious organization	Helping	Be liked
Organized workplace	Yes/no power	Solving real problems	Not supervise or manage anyone
Travel to exotic places	Be hands-on	Environment of integrity	Use analytical skills
Make $___ annually	Be the idea person	Involved in social issues	Be a #2 in the inner circle
Be an expert	Assemble teams	Work part-time	Work with smart people

Continued on next page

Solve new problems daily	Warm and fuzzy	Privy to the big picture	Opportunities to teach others
Have projects that start and end	Businesslike atmosphere	No repetitive tasks	Stability
Work with creative people	Little office politics	A new hurdle every day	Good listeners as associates
Challenging	Opportunities for learning	Able to develop new ideas	
Some predictability about what my work will be on a daily basis	Organization that is not so big you don't know what's happening	Flexibility to be creative (don't want to be told exactly how to do things)	

List your own characteristics below. Once you have written them, mark the ones that feel most important to you. You may want to look back at what energizes you and what depletes you as you make this list, paying special attention to your talents and using them in your criteria as well.

Desired characteristics of my situation

• • •

Many people have never identified what they want in life or what their criteria for joy is at work. What environments and situations enable them to do their best work? Once you are able to identify that, you will find that awareness is everything. When we are aware of what works for us, we can make our preferences known. Alternately, if we are working for ourselves, we will enter into every situation by first asking: Does this suit my criteria? How could I shift my plan so that I get to work in a way that feels satisfying? Criteria can help us focus on where we put our energies, what we say yes to, and how we strategize our lives. With the work you've done in this section, you are quickly approaching your personal summit.

CHAPTER 14

Coming Through the Clouds

Coming through the clouds means coming to a summit where possibilities are abundant. You wouldn't have made it to this place without the adventure that came before. Think back to that moment when you completed the Retrospective in Section I. From there you identified Turning Points, Characteristics, Limiting Beliefs, Gifts and Talents, and so on, finally crafting your Bull's-eye and identifying the characteristics of your ideal work situation. Each of these steps has been critical to your journey, and will lead you toward more self-aware, intentional decision making. A job that is aligned with your purpose but offers no opportunity to use your talents will leave you bored. One that uses your talents but doesn't take into account your values will leave you depressed. A life where you have achieved your desired roles but aren't living out your "Why" can leave you feeling purposeless. Each chapter and exploration was a lens that offered you a closer look into what you want now in your life.

In this chapter we are going to use all that understanding to dive into the possibilities for this next part of your life. Possibilities are, of course, infinite, but we want to know how to fit them into the glorious complexity that is uniquely you. We want to filter out what's meant for you from those options that may look attractive from a distance but aren't really what you are looking for. This helps you be crystal clear about how to Live Large.

Exploration: Putting the Jigsaw Together

Go back and look through your charts and the explorations you did in the book. Start with your Retrospective and move forward from there, scanning and remembering. As you look through all the good work you've done, ideas and notions are probably already beginning to form: *I could do this* or *I might do that* or *Wow! That seems like a possibility.*

That's exactly what we want: to generate possibilities from all that you have discovered about yourself. For some of you, scanning may be enough. You have a "sense" of what's there and what you need to remember moving forward. Others will want to make notes first and go from there.

In the following jigsaw puzzle, you will see that each piece has a title. Use the chart to fill in "your pieces." Just like with an actual puzzle, you can't see the picture until you bring the pieces together. The only one you are going to skip for now is the one titled Core Driver. We'll do that next.

1. Purpose: Your Why

2. Five Personal Characteristics from your Retrospective that will best support you moving forward

3. Five Know-Hows that energize you

4. Five Talents you love to employ

5. Your Bull's-eye statements

6. Desired Characteristics of your situation

7. Core Driver* not yet!

Here's an example, and a blank one for you to fill out:

Purpose: Your Why

Engage with creating beauty.

Core Driver

I want to teach and influence the practice of design.

Bull's-eye
My Role at Work

In my design role as a professional:

Have
- An inspiring physical space for my work
- Access to state-of-the-art design technology
- Income of $150k

Accomplish
- Design awards
- Complete Fellows Program
- Create a webinar for young people

Be
- Sought out for my creativity
- Part of a larger design community
- Influential in my field (design and design education)

Impact
- Change how design work is practiced so people with physical limitations can more fully participate

Know-Hows That Energize You

- Taking an idea from concept to reality
- Creating design collaboratives
- Mentoring younger talent
- Applying technology to design

Talents

- Translating others' ideas into visual design
- Translating ideas to reality

Personal Characteristics

- Creative
- Collaborative
- Inventive
- Like to experiment

Desired Characteristics of Your Situation

- Be a leader—not necessarily THE leader
- A visually clean workspace
- Energized colleagues
- Experimentation is valued
- New challenges and opportunities—not routine

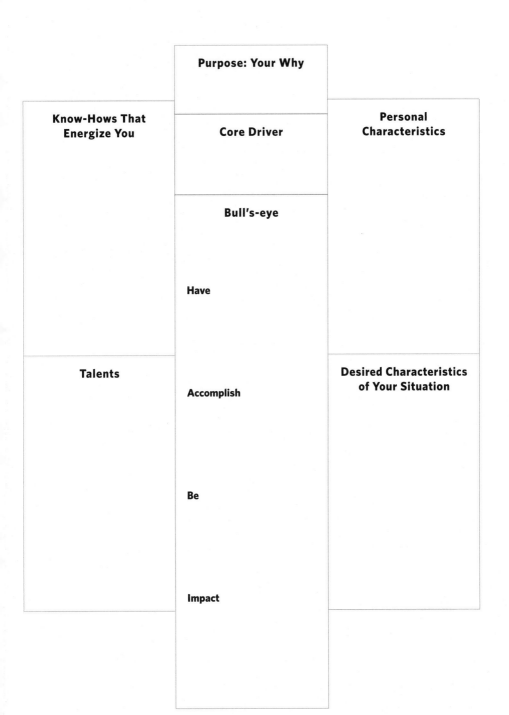

Now that you have put all the pieces together, you can see a picture that informs what's next for you. With this in hand, you can start to move toward the many possibilities of Living Large.

Exploration: Your Core Driver

It's likely that as you have worked through the book, possibilities have begun popping into your mind. *I could do this. That would be great. Wow, I realize I'd like to* . . . Is there a theme running through these possibilities? A kernel that you want to be part of your future no matter what—a *sine qua non*? In other words, what is the one thing you won't do without? This is your Core Driver.

If you take the concept of core driver and apply it to buying a house, for example, what are the most essential elements in your decision? Is it the location, the size, the price? For those of us who've gone through the house-buying process, we know it's all three. But if you must be in a certain neighborhood because of schools or work, you may compromise on size. Or if you must have four bedrooms, you may compromise on location, giving weight to that before considering other factors. Your core drivers are like that. It's what you won't move forward without.

You may say, "It's not so much the field I'm in, but the role I want to play." Maybe it's your role as a nurturer or an artist. It could be that you love working face-to-face with people. This will steer you in a different direction than if your core driver is analyzing data and coming to conclusions. Maybe it's a field you love: finance, food, wellness, energy, or education. It may be your accomplishments are the most important, or the legacy you want to leave. It could be that it doesn't matter to you what you do as long as you are serving your "Why."

Make a list of your core drivers. Some of these may repeat elements you said earlier, and that's okay. This is a final pass at what is essential for you. If you can't identify core drivers, don't worry, they are most likely woven into the things you are considering anyway. You can't fail at this. Here are a few examples:

- Be the leader

- Have location flexibility

- Work creatively on a team

- Stay in my town

- Work in _____ (name an area of interest)

Core Drivers: What I Won't Do Without

Exploration: Possibilities

Now that your core drivers are in place, it's time to generate ideas about what you are actually going to do in this next stage. We will identify the possibilities that fit you and what you want. As you come up with these possibilities, write them down in the "clouds." I like clouds more than boxes because they suggest the fluidity (not rigidity) that is still called for at this point.

If you love painting, do you want to teach it, do it, or sell it? If community service calls you, is it to give money, expertise, or hands-on work? If you have a gift for inspiring others, is it one-on-one, on a team, or are you the one on the stage?

Mary is an amazing woman who has been a philanthropist most of her life. When we met she was already sixty, and in spite of having received a sizeable inheritance when she was young, she became a doctor and moved to the rural west to serve the people in an underserved area. She had written a lot of checks in her day, but now that she was retired from medicine, she wanted to create a much higher impact. She said, "I don't want to just be a check writer, I want to be more involved." When we got to the stage of her "Core Driver" exploration, she laughed and said, "What I really want is to be an 'activist hag,' the buzzing bee, the one who gets people talking and working on an issue."

You can see how that clarity about her core driver—being a momentum builder and connector of people and issues—could inform the possibilities she pursued. Of course she also got clear about the issues and areas she wanted to impact. Now, ten years later, she has made a significant impact in her community, region, and state, and she's having the time of her life.

She hired a CEO who could manage mission-related equity investments, charitable grants, and political advocacy. She uses her resources to convene important conversations in her community and beyond. She not only invests in local business, she stimulates others in her region to do the same. She is both an activist and an activator.

As you think about your possibilities, think not only about a field or industry but about your relationship with it as well. Do you want to own it, make it, sell it, provide it, monitor it, advise it, or . . . ? Play with this. It's okay to go wild. Remember, however, that the Triple J is lurking. Don't let it discourage you from putting something (everything!) down on paper. When you hear a voice say: *"You could never be that because you're too* _____ *or not* _____ *enough,"* you know that's the Triple J.

If, for example, you know for sure you want to work in the healthcare industry—if that's one of your core drivers—your list of possibilities could be endless. The other pieces of the puzzle will help you refine your thinking.

Here is an example of the amazing number of possibilities that arise from one core driver:

Become a healthcare practitioner (nurse, physical therapist, nutrition counselor) This person's other driver might include working one-on-one, "being in the trenches," having different challenges and different opportunities to use his skills day to day, and so on.

Recruit doctors and nurses for international NGOs This person might see themselves as a connector or a big-picture thinker. She might love to travel or have a unique talent for convincing others of good causes.

Open a clinic for pregnant moms with high-risk HIV in my home city This person may have a core driver focused on community service. She might be invested in her hometown but may want to expand her horizons. Her characteristics may include leadership or being able to reach out to a diverse community of people. She may want to leave a lasting impact on her community.

Real estate broker for medical facilities This person may love business or feel happiest when his paycheck is big. He might want to be on the upper end of the growing trend in healthcare but not really want to be a healthcare provider per se.

Start a consulting firm for medical practices This person may love to work one-on-one but would like to be able to work from home and also travel domestically. He may be good at figuring out patterns and possibilities for others.

Be a volunteer coordinator in a hospital This person may be an excellent motivator who likes to have a set schedule and be part of a team at work. He may put a high value on volunteering and understand how to create bridges within an organization.

Develop software applications for patients, hospitals, doctors This person may understand and love systems like the healthcare system and want to make an impact on an overwhelmed industry that can have far-reaching effects for health and service.

Design and manufacture medical equipment This person may love engineering and be extremely creative in designing hospital equipment and knowledgeable in manufacturing processes. She may love to tinker and experiment to get something just right. However, she may not want to sell product but rather rely on someone else to get the product to market.

Create public art shows for hospitals and chronic care facilities and run retreats for artists This person may want to be connected with artists but also may be interested in serving the greater good. He may want to create art but also know for sure there's a market for it.

Be a drug company representative who makes at least $250,000 a year This person loves sales, connecting with others, making good money, traveling, and being able to count on a growing industry.

Now it's your turn to write down your possibilities! Use the clouds to write in all the jobs or careers that could be possible for you given all you now know about yourself. Write one possibility per cloud, as shown in the example below:

INDEPENDENT
GRAPHIC DESIGNER

GRAD SCHOOL

PROFESSOR AT
DESIGN SCHOOL

CORPORATE DIRECTOR
OF DESIGN

Keep brainstorming until you feel done. This does not have to be perfect, and you can always come back to add possibilities as you continue to explore.

. . .

Have an awareness of how you feel as you are writing your possibilities. Are you buoyed? Excited? Do you see how every step you have taken in the Live Large process has gotten you to this point, and that the whole of you is included in this process? Have you ever made your next career step with your whole self before, including your history, your talents, and gifts, your Know-Hows and characteristics, the roles you play, and so on? Probably not. This is a huge step. When we interact with the world using only one or a few parts of ourselves, we can begin to feel small. Now you will begin to live with your whole self, and that not only makes a larger impact on the world, it also makes you aware of how truly wide your own scope is as you move about that world. Identifying your possibilities brings you closer to what you will actually pursue. Now it's time to keep moving forward.

CHAPTER 15

The Yippee Index

If you are like me, your mind may be going in two directions at the same time. One part is saying, *wow, this would be so great!* while the other part is saying, *I don't know if this is realistic or not.* Don't worry; this is normal.

I have a client who is a wonderful man: smart, witty, a great guy. There have been times over the years when he has needed to rethink and adjust his business model. When we start brainstorming and come up with an idea, he almost immediately starts spouting forth all the reasons it won't work. Discernment is a fine thing, but not when it's premature. So to ease you through the discernment part, you'll need to use both your head and your "gut." When I say use your gut, I'm talking about using your emotions: For example, how does a possibility make you feel? It's difficult to rate your emotions, so I created a rating system I call the Yippee Index®. If a possibility makes you feel like throwing your hands up and shouting *hooray*!, rate it a five on the Yippee Index. If, on the other hand, you feel like shrugging your shoulders at a possibility, it should likely be rated a two or three on the index. Later I'll tell you the story of how the Yippee Index came to be.

Interestingly enough, I learned the power of coordinating the head and the gut to make big decisions from my son Rob, who has been a white-water paddler since his teens. He paddles Class Five rapids—stuff no mother should ever have to see her offspring do. When he was not paddling out west or in foreign countries, the Green River outside Hendersonville, North Carolina, was one of his frequent runs. One day, he had just come back from a day on the river, and I was grateful to have him safe and sound. "How'd it go?" I asked.

"I paddled Gorilla today. It's been three years since I took that one on. It's an unbelievable run. The full volume of the river funnels into a five-foot slot leading into a turbulent pool ten feet from a twenty-foot waterfall. And the safe landing spot is the size of a small coffee table! To be successful, you have to be able to improvise—from plan A to plan D."

Horrified at the thought and relieved he was back, I was also curious: "Since you've done it in the past, what took you so long to do it again, and why today?"

He replied patiently, "When you approach a difficult rapid, you first walk the bank to assess the situation and ask yourself the following questions:

- Is there a path through the rapid?
- Do I have the skill to execute the maneuvers required to run that path?

- If I fail to execute, can I get out alive?

- And last you check your gut. 'How am I feeling today?'

If you get a 'yes' to all the questions, you run the rapid. And once you enter, you stay entirely focused on what you are doing. You don't second-guess or reconsider: you trust your instinct."

I immediately recognized, and I'm sure you do too, how well this reasoning applies to many moments in life that could be considered high risk.

The lesson I take from how Rob walked the bank was that when it comes to finding what's next, I have to assess the situation and my ability to execute. If I want to be a guide in Glacier National Park, I can't just show up. I first have to carefully assess the situation—in other words, I have to use my head. At the same time, there comes a moment when all the facts, data, pros and cons get put away, and I must check in with my gut as well: How do I feel?

This "gut check" is the Yippee Index. I came up with the Yippee Index one afternoon when I was working with a bright intellectual properties lawyer in the music industry. She had become increasingly frustrated with her boss, who was difficult to work with, and the dog-eat-dog environment he had created. She wasn't sure what her options were, so together we brainstormed as many possibilities as we could: Join another music rights organization, join a record label, start her own law firm, join an existing law firm, shift to government relations work (she loved politics), seek staff work with a senator or representative . . . the list went on. To help her narrow down her choices, I said: "When you look at these options, which one makes you want to say 'Yippee!'?" That's how the Yippee Index rating was born.

"Yippee!" is an expression that harkens back to a time of greater innocence, a time when it was okay to jump up and shout with glee—no judgment, no holding back, arms raised in the air. This index is to help you discern which of your options may be right for you.

Exploration: Assessing Your Options

In this exploration we will look at the benefits and risks for each possibility (your head), and then rate each on the Yippee Index (your gut), a scale of one to five, with five being the highest in the index—the possibilities that have you saying "Yippee!" the loudest. Once you do this, you may realize that some of the possibilities are not worth pursuing, and that's okay.

In the chart on p.166:

1. List each possibility you identified in the previous chapter.

2. List the benefits of each possibility. Ask yourself: Why is this a good option? What good consequences or opportunities may open up with this option (e.g., a chance to learn new things, meet people who share your interests, and earn more money)? Benefits may also refer to how well the possibility matches the criteria you identified in Chapter 13. For example, some of your possibilities may allow you to travel more, or not have to travel as much, be on a team, be the boss, or be able to work from different locations.

3. List the risks/disadvantages of each possibility. These may include low job security, low pay, or that the position may require another degree.

4. Now rate each possibility. Which one makes you feel like saying, "Yippee!"? Rate this a five. When you feel "Yippee!" about a possibility, it gives you energy to pursue it.

5. For each possibility that you want to pursue, write down what the next steps might be. This may include things like:

   a. Call Joe and have him introduce me to Sam at ABC company

   b. Do online research about firms in my area

   c. Identify licensing requirements in my state

   d. Make an appointment for an information interview with Jean Jones, president of XYZ company

. . . and so on.

For those possibilities with a high Yippee Index, you may have lots of next steps in mind. Don't feel overwhelmed by this! What matters most for now is the first next step—your next green light as you begin your journey toward your possibility.

Here is a sample of what your chart might look like:

Possibilities	Benefits	Risks/ disadvantages	Yippee Index	Next steps
Independent graphic designer	• Make my own hours • I get to create things • Do my own designs	• Have to constantly look for new business • Money is unpredictable	2	• None
Designer at ABC advertising	• Work with other professionals • Be part of a team • Stable income	• Don't know what kind of accounts I would have • Been there, done that	2	• None
Professor at design school	• Love to teach others • Have professional colleagues • Could learn more about delivering material online	• Don't know what the opportunities are for me to do my own design work • 30-mile commute	4	• Contact local school to learn about their programs and requirements for teaching
Known expert— offer online courses	• Time/place flexibility • Teaching can be very profitable • I get to create things • Would eventually have time to create my own designs	• Would need to learn about how to deliver and make money • Working alone?	4	• Research current offerings • Identify their audience • See where there is a gap in the market

Possibilities	Benefits	Risks/ disadvantages	Yippee Index	Next steps
Corporate director of design	• Reputation builder, national scope • Could mentor young designers • Good comp and benefits • Could be a launching pad for my own thing (online courses, running own my department)	• Corporate politics? • Would I have the opportunity to do my own designs? • Don't know about local opportunities	4	• Set up information interviews: Companies with design departments (contact their heads) • Prep questions I want to ask
Grad school	• I love learning new things • Increases the strength of my knowledge base • Helps me better understand trends and technology • Positions me to be an "expert"	• Costs money • Is this the right time at this point in my career?	4+	• Identify the appropriate graduate offerings, cost, and time requirements • Are there low-residency programs or programs locally?

Core driver: I want to teach and influence the practice of design.

Possibilities	Benefits	Risks/ disadvantages	Yippee index	Next steps

Core driver:

• • •

In Stephen Covey's best-selling book, *The 7 Habits of Highly Effective People*, he talks about the difference between urgent and important. "Urgent" refers to all the tasks that have to be done now, in the short term—for example, going to the grocery store today, because you don't have food in the house. "Important" refers to those things that can have a significant impact but may not be time bound—for example, meeting with your family to plan how you can make your meals and mealtime healthier. Because you can theoretically complete these important tasks at any time, they tend to get postponed.

Answering your email can feel urgent. Planning how to use an assistant to make better use of your own time is important. And yes, you can have things that are both urgent and important—like calling the police because someone is breaking in! And sometimes things feel urgent that are truly not important—like answering a text when you are having a face-to-face conversation with a friend. Covey advises that we spend enough time on important things even if they aren't urgent and to be selective in responding to the urgent things when they are not important. It's easy to let "urgent" take precedence over "important." Taking your next steps is important. It's up to you to make them urgent.

This is illustrated in the story about the professor who came into class one day with a large jar filled with rocks. He asked his students if the jar was full. They replied yes, indeed it was full. He then poured gravel into the same jar, and it filled in around the rocks. He then said, "Is the jar full now?" The students quickly agreed that yes, now the jar really was full. Then the professor poured sand into the jar that held the rocks and the gravel and asked the students once more if the jar was full. Yes, they agreed, the jar was now truly full.

"So students," he said, "what is the lesson you take from this?" No one spoke. The professor said, "The jar is like the time you have available in your life. The rocks symbolize the most important things you can do with your time. The gravel is next, but clearly less important. And the sand . . . well, it's just filler. But what would happen if I filled the jar with sand first? There wouldn't be any room for the rocks, for the important things."

So it is with our lives. The rocks represent the important things: time with family and friends, learning new things, or creating plans for your future. The sand represents that which is neither important nor urgent: playing games on your tablet, watching mind-numbing TV, or seeking perfection for situations that don't matter (who cares if all the paper cups for the picnic match?). If we fill our days, lives, and calendars with "sand," there won't be room for the rocks. Are you willing to make your move toward a richer life that makes you say "Yippee," an important priority—a "rock"? If yes, then treat it as such. That means putting that first step on your calendar right now.

Exploration: Making Your Future a Priority

Your next steps are not going on a "to-do" list. We all have these lists, and most of us know how things have a way of taking up residence on them and never moving. Instead, let's do something much better.

1. Write out a sentence that describes the outcome or results you want to create. Express it as if it were already true: "The book manuscript is ready for review," "The business

plan is in front of investors," "The website is live," "My new job has started." Results and outcomes don't have to be big: "The executive summary for my business idea is complete," "The project budget is developed," "Chapter 3 is complete," "Three information interviews are scheduled." The assumption is that any of these outcomes requires many steps to reach completion. That's why you can't just put them on a to-do list!

2. Write down the date by which you hope to be engaged in the work, project, or role you want to be in. It may take one month, one year, or longer.

3. On your calendar, block time segments each week when you are going to focus on actions that will create the outcome you want (hint: I do mine on Friday morning or Sunday afternoon). This is something I learned from Tony Robbins.

4. Pick a label for that block of time. One that, when you see it, will reconnect you with the excitement you have for making it come true! For example: My Future, My Book, My Next Chapter . . .

You may not yet know the specific tasks you are going to address in that block of time, and that's okay. It may be creating an outline, making phone calls, scheduling appointments, doing research, taking a class, or buying supplies and equipment. What you do know is that you have reserved the time: You've made it a priority to move toward your outcome.

Working this way, you'll be amazed how your gradual progress every week moves you closer and closer to what you want to be, have, and accomplish, and closer to making the impact you want to make. Use the following chart to help guide you:

My outcome or result: My new role!	**Completion date:** 3/31/XX
I'm engaged in a new situation that satisfies me and pays me well	

Weekly outcome:
Have information from the design school.

Tasks:	**Time required:** 90 mins
Identify area schools; contact each for faculty requirements	
	On the calendar: Yes

Weekly outcome:
Four companies with design departments are identified and a contact for each

Tasks:	**Time required:** 90 mins
Get list of largest employers in my area; get list of top employers	
	On the calendar: Yes

Weekly outcome:

Tasks:	**Time required:**
	On the calendar:

My outcome or result:	Completion date:	
Weekly outcome:		
Tasks:	**Time required:**	
	On the calendar:	
Weekly outcome:		
Tasks:	**Time required:**	
	On the calendar:	
Weekly outcome:		
Tasks:	**Time required:**	
	On the calendar:	

• • •

In those moments of self-doubt (and we all have them), review your talents, purpose, and values, and let them reinspire you. When you feel mired in the details, remind yourself of the impact you want to make. If the Triple J has been whispering in your ear, go back to the Limiting Beliefs section and see what beliefs you may still be holding dear that you are ready to let go of. And come back and visit me on the website www.elizabethbcrook.com. It's a place to remind yourself of all you have to offer!

CHAPTER 16

Coming Through Your Yikes

You are at an incredible apex. You've learned who you are, broken through limitations, and identified so many possibilities. So, why do we sometimes get to this point and find ourselves saying: "Ready, Set, Set, Set . . ." and then we never actually "Go"? Why do we get cold feet or sweaty palms when we think about what going for the life we want implies?

Several years ago when I began writing this book, my editor Suzanne encouraged me to participate in the National Publicity Summit in New York, an event that brings together writers, speakers, and other experts with over a hundred media representatives from broadcast, print, and online media. She encouraged me, "This is a chance to connect with outlets who want to interview you about your book. It's important to establish yourself as the expert you are!"

Even as Suzanne was reminding me that I have a unique voice

and a process that has inspired many people to make significant and positive changes in their lives, the voice in my head kept saying, "*Yikes!*" She wanted me to pitch myself to executive producers and editors, talk-show hosts, and freelance bloggers. I felt overwhelmed, inadequate, and afraid. How could I possibly do this?

The excuses I gave myself were overwhelming. Like many of you, I was raised to "not be too big for my britches" or think I was a big deal. Being humble and self-diminishing was the preferred way to go, right? The book wasn't even finished—if I told all my stories and gave away my ideas, who would buy the book . . . *right?* And besides, if I were "out there," people might think I was putting myself on a pedestal, "putting on airs." And that extra weight I had planned on losing? How could I be on television if I weren't the size of a talk show host?

The Triple J is the voice we hear that tells us we can't or we shouldn't. Our Yikes, on the other hand, is our own voice expressing the doubt and fear the Triple J has inspired. Clearly, my Triple J was going crazy, but before it sent me running to hide under the bed, I stopped. Here's how you can stop your own Triple J.

How to Stop a Runaway Triple J

Have you ever been driving on a highway with a mountain grade? That means the road is steep enough that your car will go downhill without your touching the accelerator. There are caution signs and speed limits for trucks because anything that big and heavy can build up a momentum that can get out of control. If the brakes should fail? Disaster! That's why these roads have runaway truck ramps, designed to slow down the truck so the driver can regain control and safely stop the vehicle before he or she runs off the road and causes serious damage. After all, the driver's goal is to deliver the cargo to its destination, returning the truck and himself safely to home base.

The Triple J can be like a runaway truck. If you can't stop it safely, it can take you off the road and down into a ditch, so it's important to have a runaway ramp that can bring you back to safety.

The best way to stall a runaway Triple J is to ask yourself some questions. Questions have a way of slowing us down and giving us time to think and recover. That's why the best coaches, salespeople, teachers, and friends ask questions. It's why I ask you so many questions in the book. It's why your ability to ask yourself questions is so important.

> The first question you must ask yourself to stop the Triple J is this: "What am I trying to accomplish?" "What is the outcome I want to achieve?"

When my editor suggested that I meet a hundred of the most influential media people in the country in order to bring my book into the public eye, I had to go back to my outcome. What did I want?

- I want to help people Live Large in their work.

- I want to have a successful book.

- Would attending the National Publicity Summit allow me to do that? *Yes!* But I would have to do some things that initially scared me. So I also asked myself: "What am I afraid of?"

- I don't want to look or feel ridiculous.

- I don't want to be rejected.

- I'm afraid I don't know how to pitch myself.

I could go on and on. I have an energetic Triple J, but you get the picture. And then I asked this most important question: Are there resources (both internal and external) to help me? *Yes!* I will have to seek out and ask for help. I will have to gain some skill and experience with new tools. I will have to be willing to feel and, indeed, be less than expert and skillful for some period of time. But I can do it. Is getting to my outcome worth dealing with my fear? You better believe it! Will the Triple J be there along the way? Of course. But I (and you) have tools for dealing with it.

Stop and Ask Questions:

- What am I trying to accomplish—what is my outcome?

- What am I afraid of? Remember, sometimes it's the fear of feeling inadequate that stops us, not an insurmountable inadequacy.

- What resources do I have?

- Is my outcome worth it?

Jot down your answers. Read them again. Getting to where we want will mean recognizing the "Yikes," then doing it anyway.

I could do this! How did I know? Because I'd done it before. In order to gain the confidence, I needed to move into this new phase of exposure to big media outlets. I thought back to all those things I'd once thought were impossible but had somehow managed to pull off: I'd learned a second language at thirty, started to ski at fifty, founded my own company, and had many, many more beautiful successes. Knowing I'd had success before allowed me to know that I could have greater success now.

The same is true for you.

Exploration: Getting Through Your Yikes

In order to get through your Yikes and onto your Yippee, it can help to count the successes you have already had—times you've made it through your Yikes.

As you were putting events on your Lifeline, you no doubt recalled some memories of when you felt the odds were against you, when you had to push, or when you weren't sure you could accomplish what you did: a time when you said "Yikes!" but moved forward anyway.

Having worked with many smart, successful, talented people like you over the years, the thing I see most often is that most of us minimize how resourceful we've been. We have already achieved success many times. At one point these successes were only a hope or a dream. Tony Robbins introduced me to this way of thinking. He often says we must create certainty in our own minds so we can do what seems impossible or only a dream. This exploration is designed to help you remember how good you already are at doing that.

To help you with this exploration, here are some examples from my list:

Became Bilingual at Age Thirty, When I Moved to Latin America

When I decided to move to Venezuela, not learning Spanish was simply not an option. My ability to find my place and create a life depended on it.

Actions I Took:

- Made a commitment

- Got expert help

- Practiced every day with my teacher

- Adopted the method to suit what I knew about my own learning style

- Did the practices—told the stories over and over

- Spoke even if I wasn't perfect

- Allowed myself to be a beginner

Started a Business

As a former executive, being a businesswoman and a professional was—and continues to be—an important role for me.

Actions I Took:

- Didn't let failure become an option

- Started with the first green light

- Kept track of my money

- Networked

- Got expert help and mentors

- Kept refining and redefining

- Focused on MY strengths

- Used my network and reputation

- Stopped grasping

- Stopped expecting others to "be the solution"

- Put in professional systems

Wrote a Book

I wanted to write a book because I wanted to use my knowledge and experience to help people. My Why is to help others fulfill *their* Why, their purpose.

Actions I Took:

- Made a commitment

- Got a coach

- Made sure I had sources of support and encouragement

- Did it little by little

- Set aside times of intense work

- Didn't fret about perfection

- Used assistance in cleaning it up

- Anticipated the deadlines

Now, take a minute and note in the chart three successes you've had. For *each one*, write down the actions you took or the conditions in play that led to your being successful.

Successes I've had	Actions that led to success
1.	1. 2. 3. 4. 5.
2.	1. 2. 3. 4. 5.
3.	1. 2. 3. 4. 5.

Notice the actions you have taken to meet challenges or reach achievements. Are there themes or patterns? What have you learned about how *you* achieve success? Now, close your eyes, take a deep breath, and consider what advice you have for yourself in light of what you have learned. Remember, you already know things that have worked for you in the past. This is simply a time to recall them.

Advice to my future self:

• • •

Remember that whatever you are attempting, you have been on this cliff's edge before, and many, many times you have come away flying.

CHAPTER 17

Standing on the Precipice of Change

You are now standing on the precipice of change. You've come to know yourself in a whole new way, and the path leading you toward the next chapter of your life lies before you. You've not only embraced your talents, you've learned to distinguish the voice of the Triple J from your own good counsel, and you've just remembered all those actions you have taken to deal with and create change—change that has helped you achieve. Yet, anytime there's change, fear is close behind.

We've all heard the common refrain: Change is the only constant in life. But even when changes are exciting—we get married, have a child, hit a financial windfall, or attain sudden fame—they can also be disorienting. More often than not, the consequences of *not* changing, or making the "safer" choice, are often greater than making the choice to embrace the big, challenging, all-encompassing changes that await us.

My dear friend Lydia, the daughter of Holocaust survivors, learned this when she was still a little girl. Her grandmother lived in a big house in Latvia with her extended family. When they started hearing rumors of what was happening to other Jewish families, her grandmother said, in effect: "Don't be ridiculous: As long as we stay put, we'll be fine." They didn't see the wave that was coming. The only survivor was Lydia's mother. The fear of changing cost her family their lives.

Most of us overrate the difficulty and inconvenience of change rather than taking a hard look at the cost of not changing. Lydia's story might be dramatic, but countless stories demonstrate that people in business and life seeking less risk or attempting to keep things the same may inadvertently expose themselves to more risk or create more chaos for themselves.

When you are afraid to take the next step and find yourself hesitating, one of the best, hardest, and most revealing questions to ask yourself is this: What are the costs of not changing? What are the new or unintentional risks I may be creating in order to feel safe?

When I was in my midforties, my son Rob took me rock climbing in Boulder, Colorado, for the first time. Rob had been climbing for a number of years, so I figured he knew what he was doing when he told me he had a climb picked out for us. We set off on a Saturday morning. After hiking an hour and a half up rugged talus slopes, we finally reached the base of the Flatirons—sandstone rock formations that rise vertically more than a thousand feet. We were surrounded by tall evergreens and rocks that towered above us. A strong line connected the climbing harnesses around our waists. Rob helped me gear up and gave me instructions about how we would ascend, and what I would need to pay attention to.

In a two-person climb, the lead climber goes first, while the bottom climber belays him. This technique provides security for the climbers—they can only fall the length of rope. It's still a long way, but at least we wouldn't die!

Rob reached the first pitch and "hooked in" to the rock, then called down, "On belay, climb on." As I started up and cleared the trees, I could see I was already several hundred feet off the valley floor. By the time I reached Rob, I was nauseous with fear.

"How ya doing, Mom?" he asked.

"I am really scared," I replied.

"Don't you know you're safe? We are tied in, and since I'm leading, you can't fall."

"Yes," I replied, "but I still feel shaky."

He suggested we stay there until I felt ready. After a few minutes, with breathing and conversation, I felt secure enough to move on. We repeated the process. When he finished his next pitch, he called me to begin my next ascent and coached me up the immense sandstone face, reminding me to use my feet and legs for support. As I concentrated on the technical requirements of the climb, I began to focus less and less on how high we were.

Again I reached Rob, we talked for a few minutes, then he began to climb. And so we went, until we had repeated the sequence some four times. I was nearing the top, buoyed with a sense of accomplishment and charged with adrenaline. As I prepared to start the last pitch, my awareness of how high I truly was reemerged—and so did my fear. I started looking into a vertical funnel in the rock, a little carved-out nook that looked safe, protected, and secure. As I headed into it, Rob called out, "Don't go in there, Mom!" It was too late. I had moved into what climbers call a chimney and was stuck. Unable to come down, I was faced with climbing an overhang—a difficult maneuver that required a fair amount of upper body strength. It took most of what was left of my stamina. At last I made it to the top, shaking but triumphant.

Later, as Rob and I were talking about the climb, I reflected on how hard it had been to get out of that chimney. Rob said, "It's tempting to climb inside a chimney because it gives you a feeling of security and safety, relieving the sense of exposure you experience hanging on the rock face . . . but it is false security. It took more effort to climb out of the chimney than it would have if you had just moved up the open face, in spite of your fear."

In seeking security and a way out of our fear, we often create greater hardship for ourselves and end up having to face the very thing we were trying to avoid in the first place. What looks like the safer path, the one that will reduce our fears, may be the path less likely to lead to our success or happiness. That "safe" path keeps us in uninspiring careers, jobs, even relationships that don't have us saying "Yippee." After finishing *Live Large*, you may realize how far you have come, how high up you really are. It's critical you face your fears and fight against the urge to go back to your safe path.

Some of the fear you have when it comes to taking the next step is failing to realize how much you have changed. One of my clients, Thea, came to me in her fifties. Over the past thirty years she'd become an expert in her industry, especially in developing profitable, long-term client relationships. She wanted to explore other career options, but one of the first things she said to me was that she'd never gone to college. She hadn't considered how much she'd changed: Not having a college degree was no longer the make-or-break issue it had been when she was twenty-one.

Endless possibilities lay ahead in her future that didn't require a college degree, but her fear prohibited her from seeing them.

You have changed, too, since the last time you took a "next step." What's different? Inevitably, you have places in your life where you have grown, expanded, know more, and have more to give. Your urgency to buy this book may be because somewhere you weren't living as if you had changed. You were "living small," not realizing that what once mattered doesn't anymore, that you can start on a new path, no longer rooted in something someone told you way back when.

Buying this book was a sign that you are ready to let go of that old way of being.

And this will keep happening. *You* will keep happening. Years ago someone told me life is like a spiral. Unlike a circle, which keeps you going around and around, a spiral looks more like a mountain road. As we weave our way up the mountain, we see the same view over and over again, but each time we are seeing it from a different perspective. That changing perspective lets us know how high we've climbed. There is a word for that: *iteration.* Although this word can mean repetition, the definition listed that speaks to me is: *A new version of something.* That's what you are becoming. This journey is your next iteration. And through all of the completed explorations in this book, you have finally come to know that you are ready for it.

CHAPTER 18

Lessons from Valerie's Happy Restroom

I remember my last morning during my trip to Fiji, I awoke early in order to catch my last sunrise in paradise. More than one hundred yards off the beach was a long coral reef where the incoming waves break. The sound of the breaking waves had sung me to sleep every night. Because the waves break so far away from shore, the ocean close to shore is quiet and clear. This morning, as the sky was glowing pink and orange, I was struck by how placid the surface of the water was. It looked more like a lake. In that instance an insect or small fish, too small for me to see, broke the surface. It sent ripples out across the water. Then another creature created its own epicenter, and then another. In the blink of an eye, the surface in front of me was shimmering.

Our actions can have a similar impact. As individuals we send ripples across the tidal pool of our families, our communities, and indeed even farther. In listening to people over the years, almost everyone I have ever worked with has expressed a desire to give back or make a difference in their community or in the world. I have come to believe the need for service is probably universal. It may seem, as you complete this book, that it's all been about one person: you. For some that may feel uncomfortable, even selfish. You may have struggled through some of the book, feeling like you were spending too much time on yourself instead of considering others.

Here's the happy truth: Your living your full purpose and using your talents are the greatest gifts you can give the world. Think of Gandhi and his famous quote, "Be the change you wish to see in the world."

Knowing where your talents lie and what you are good at, being clear about your values and what energizes you, will allow you the energy to give back in big and small ways. When my house was almost completely destroyed by fire in the late, 90s, Aimee, a young woman who worked at the YWCA where I was a volunteer, appeared in front of the charred remains and said, "You are going to need help with all sorts of things, like calling the utilities, saving your accounting, and having a space to work and a computer to use. I am good at those things. Let me help."

My sometimes-handyman Eugene also lent a hand. I say "sometimes" because sometimes he was drunk, sometimes he was in jail, sometimes he was womanizing. But Eugene knew what he was good at and how he could help. After the fire was no longer a danger, he helped move out what could be salvaged and put it in the shed. And, to prevent looting, he stayed in the house until it could be boarded up and made secure.

It's easy in Western culture to be seduced by the notion that you have to have big bucks, like Bill Gates, Warren Buffett, and other billionaires who have pledged to give significant parts of their fortunes to help humanity and the glorious and fragile planet that is our home. In reality, giving back on any level is an important source of inspiration as you move forward. When we think solely of ourselves, we can get mired in thoughts of unworthiness or self-doubt. But when we think of working for the greater good, the motivation tends to rise like wildfire.

Icestone is a manufacturing company located in the Brooklyn Navy Yard. They make a beautiful, durable surface product—think countertops, floors, and walls from 100% recycled glass. That in itself is huge. Imagine the millions of tons of bottles that are taken out of the waste stream, thanks to their work! In addition to that, their factory is "day lit," therefore it uses less electricity. They recycle their wastewater. They provide good jobs to inner-city residents, hire political refugees, offer ESL (English as a Second Language) courses, have an ethnically diverse workforce, and offer employees a financial stake in the company. *Wow!*

Village Real Estate in Nashville, Tennessee, chose to focus on the greater good by supporting the vitality of the city's existing neighborhoods. A real-estate development company, Village repurposes old manufacturing spaces close to downtown into exciting and vibrant places to live and work. The Village Fund has given away one million dollars to neighborhood organizations. Most agents pledge an amount to the fund for every sale they make. They've also partnered with the city to encourage homeowners to do an energy audit of their homes.

It may be that giving back is integrated into the roles you play. Meredith, a friend of mine in her fifties, began mentoring a young woman some dozen years ago. In the course of time, her mentee got pregnant and had a son named Sam. Sam is now in his preteen years. During his summer vacation, Sam lives with Meredith and her husband during the week. This gives his mom a break and allows her to keep her job. It also means Sam gets to experience a whole side of life that he might otherwise never see.

In doing this work, we all have the power to make a difference in the world, beginning right now. It just takes intention and attention. Take a moment to think of the needs in the world that pull at your heart. Make sure that you factor them into your next step. It could be in the role you play in your family, the way your product or service benefits your community, or how you are able to shift one tiny piece of your daily life toward others: taking your elderly neighbor's paper to her front porch, letting the car in front of you go first, offering to help before being asked. How do you feel when you think of your next step as something that gives back to the wider world?

Valerie's Happy Restroom, or It Doesn't Have to Be Big to Be Big

Recently I was in the Charlotte, NC, airport: Concourse C. Tired and wishing I had had a direct flight from Winston-Salem to Nashville, I went to the ladies' room. As I walked in, a voice rang out, "Welcome to Valerie's happy restroom! Come on in, ladies. Have I got a seat for you!" The airport bathroom had hand lotion, mints, and other niceties worthy of the Ritz-Carlton.

I smiled with the utter unexpectedness of it all. Women were chatting as they washed their hands and smiling as they shared "road warrior" tales. We all chuckled as Valerie sang out her greeting again and again while making sure everything was neat and in order.

Intrigued, I approached Valerie and asked her how she happened to be here on C concourse, doing what she was doing. She smiled and told me her story. She had been laid off from another job several years before. She tried to find work in her field, but there were no jobs to be had. She asked a friend of hers who worked at the airport if she might find something there. All they had were part-time jobs as restroom attendants. She took the job and enjoyed it so much that she moved to full time when the opportunity came.

Curious, I asked, "What are the best parts of your job?"

She happily responded, "When I started working here, I saw so many women—young and old, moms and grannies, and business ladies like you—and so many of them looked tired, beat down, and grumpy. They seemed like they needed a pick-me-up. Every day I get to put a smile on someone's face. It just makes me feel good."

I continued, "Are you on this concourse and gate every day?"

"Oh no, ma'am," she replied. "I just go where the good Lord tells me they need a little happiness."

As Valerie energetically went on with her work, I thought, *This is such an important part of leading lives we love: being able to find the meaning and joy in work we do, no matter what it is.*

Does that mean we have to "settle" to just make lemonade out of lemons? Not at all! The point is that, while we may believe that what makes our heart sing has to be big, noble, and earth changing, living a rich life is really just about finding what Valerie found: meaning, a sense of accomplishment, and yes, joy. When we tap into those things, we grow, and doors that we might not imagine will open for us.

Will Valerie start an airport happiness service, create a franchise model, go public, and make a million dollars? Probably not. Will she use the energy her work generates to do more things that increase her Yippee Index? You can count on that.

It's so easy to get stuck looking for the one big thing. Don't. Remember Valerie. I'll be in the Charlotte airport soon, and I'll be looking for her.

Dr. Seuss and Never Saying Good-bye

Now, with the rest of the book behind you and your journey complete, you have revitalized goals and plans. You have enhanced understanding of yourself and know how to leverage all of who you are. You have tools for getting back on track when you wander off. You are certainly at *an* ending . . . not *the* ending.

With all endings come new beginnings and new endings and so on. The notion of the life/death/life cycle is common to all religions and spiritual practices: Like the yoga teacher Rodney Yee told me, we begin, and we begin again and again. We too often tend to cling to the notion of completion and perfection—of "being done." This is an illusion that keeps us from the richness of the moment and of the larger process.

If you are a gardener, you know that gardens evolve not only each day but each season. And so it is in our lives. What is exciting or challenging at one season in our lives ceases to be so in another. The process of transformation never ends. We are all unfinished— and that's a good thing.

When I lived in Caracas, I came to know an extraordinary psychotherapist, Lila Lee Scott (Vega). I had heard her give a talk at the American Embassy and was attracted to her clear thinking and her practical approach. In my midthirties, like many others, I became aware of unresolved issues that were getting in my way— patterns of thought and behavior that were creating anxiety and frustration. I sought out Dr. Vega, as she was known at the time, and asked if she would take me as a patient. Like in the movies, I would go to her office and lie down on her couch and talk. The insights and discoveries I made about myself were significant. Sometimes I thought of the process as cleaning out the drawers in the dresser of my subconscious. As we went deeper, I realized I had drawers that I hadn't even realized were there. There were times when I would ask Lila, "Are there still more drawers or have we gotten to the last one? *Am I done, fixed, perfect?*" I don't think she ever gave me an answer.

My work with her was an experience that has had significant impact on my life. The part I want to share here at the end of this book is this: There is no such thing as cleaning out all the drawers! We can pull them out and tidy them up and close them, leaving good order, but when we least expect it, one of those drawers, with its attendant "issues," can pop open again. So the goal is not to get rid of our imperfections. The goal is to be able to recognize our own limiting patterns when they come up—and then choose something else. The goal is to expand our options for action— what I call expanding our repertoire of responses. You may think of it as your wardrobe of responses. So even if your favorite outfit is jeans and a tee-shirt, you want to be able to pick a different outfit when the situation calls for it: a swimsuit for the beach, a parka for the slopes! When you are able to recognize an unproductive behavior or thought pattern, you can say: *Ah, there you are. Do you serve me well or not? Do I want to take you out and use you, or shall I just put you away?*

Living Large does not mean never feeling uncomfortable, angry, or frustrated. It doesn't mean your life will come together into a neat and tidy package. Living Large means intentionally choosing the ways in which we live and work—and not being afraid to choose the ways that bring us toward a richer, fuller world.

In closing, remember the words of that great philosopher Dr. Seuss:

> You have Brains in your Head.
> You have Feet in your Shoes.
> You can Steer yourself any
> Direction you Choose.

ACKNOWLEDGMENTS

First and foremost, I'd like to thank the people who early on sought my help in figuring out what was next for them. Their willingness to explore their own lives created opportunities for them and for me.

Thanks to Lisa Quin Lorimer Donahue, who not only encouraged me to just "write the damn book" but also introduced me to Suzanne Kingsbury, book shaman and development editor *extraordinaire*, whose unflagging enthusiasm, confidence, and skill made me a better writer and this a better book. She is the *sine qua non* of *Live Large*.

Along with Lisa, Dawn McGee has been a friend and writing buddy of mine from early on. For many years, my monthly calls with these women have kept me moving when I might have otherwise given up.

I am also grateful for my larger community of friends whose love, support, patience, and judgment-free "haven't you finished the book yet?" questions have buoyed me along. Among others, these friends include Nan Allison, Jan Brandes, Martha Burton, Pam

Chaloult, Meg Donahue, Kathleen Harkey, Joel Solomon, and my BCGY group Dana Wilde, Pat Obuchowski, and Shari Spencer.

Thanks to Joann Akers for her enthusiastic and nonjudgmental listening that encouraged my writing decades before I knew I had books to write.

Thanks to my children—Rob and Katie Howell, Sarah and Aracelis Fontana—and their families.

The early enthusiasm of my sisters—Nancy Crook Ward and Cynthia Crook—was critical, as was the model my father William G. Crook, MD, gave me when he published a million-copy best-seller at age sixty-nine.

Books of this sort invariably rest on the influence of mentors and others. Conversations with Jack Canfield and Tony Robbins both challenged and encouraged me. Lila Lee Scott, MD, and Susan Austin Crumpton, both skilled and compassionate therapists, helped me get out of my own way and provided ideas that helped shape powerful sections on limiting beliefs. My personal coach Cindy Rold has consistently given me back the power I always had to take charge of my own life.

Thanks to my generous friends Pat Shea, Nicky Weaver, and Joel Solomon, who invited me to use their houses or apartments in beautiful tranquil places to write in peace.

The team at Orchard Advisors has made this journey possible in spite of heavy workloads and changing circumstances. Joni Sasaki Kane, my long-time assistant, has managed huge segments of my business and my life to give me time to write. Heidi Hartman, momentum manager, has been the source of all manner of wisdom, humor, and practicality. She is integral to the impact we will have in changing people's lives. Jill Dahl is a recent and valuable addition who brings energy and expertise in helping us get the word out!

I never understood why authors so frequently mentioned their publishers, but now I do. The team at Greenleaf Book Group has been key in bringing this work to its current form—thanks to Kat Fatland, my talented copy editor, and Jen Glynn, who kept the project on track, as well as the rest of the Greenleaf team, including Scott James and Neil Gonzalez.

Thanks also to the team at Bradley Communications: to Steve Harrison for teaching us how to make a book successful; to Geoffrey Berwin for storytelling; and to Martha Bullen for wisdom and advice making the book publisher-ready.

Last but not least, thank you to the love of my life Umberto Fontana, who challenged me when I was still in my twenties to Live Large. His love, encouragement, and daily support—from cooking to shopping to foot rubs—have made it all possible.

Umberto José Fontana Briceño died March 6, 2017 as this book was going to print. His death serves as a poignant invitation to Live Large now. As he was fond of saying, *This is no dress rehearsal.*

EBC—Nashville, March 10, 2017

ABOUT THE AUTHOR

Elizabeth Crook is the CEO of Orchard Advisors, where entrepreneurs, business and community leaders, and philanthropists turn when they want to Live Large and grow both their enterprises and their impact. Elizabeth holds a BA from Vanderbilt University and an MS from Tennessee State University. A mother, grandmother, and ardent hiker, she lives on Music Row in Nashville with the love of her life, Umberto. Elizabeth believes that if we all loved our work, we could change the world! *Live Large* is her first book.